Digital Marketing

Digital Marketing

COMMUNICATING, SELLING AND CONNECTING

Charles F. Hofacker

Carl DeSantis Professor of Business Administration, College of Business, Florida State University, USA

Edward Elgar
PUBLISHING

Cheltenham, UK • Northampton, MA, USA

Published by
Edward Elgar Publishing Limited
The Lypiatts
15 Lansdown Road
Cheltenham
Glos GL50 2JA
UK

Edward Elgar Publishing, Inc.
William Pratt House
9 Dewey Court
Northampton
Massachusetts 01060
USA

A catalogue record for this book
is available from the British Library

Library of Congress Control Number: 2018931792

MIX
Paper from
responsible sources
FSC
www.fsc.org   FSC® C013056

ISBN 978 1 78811 534 6 (cased)
ISBN 978 1 78811 536 0 (paperback)
ISBN 978 1 78811 535 3 (eBook)

Typeset by Servis Filmsetting Ltd, Stockport, Cheshire
Printed and bound in Great Britain by TJ International Ltd, Padstow, Cornwall

Contents in brief

SECTION IV   DIGITAL NETWORKS AS A CONNECTION SERVICE

Full contents

Preface

Dear Students,

I began writing this book in July, 2008 and used it for the first time in draft form during the semester starting in September, 2008. I believe this book and the distribution system I've chosen for it represents a potential way to curb the rising cost of textbooks, and I also believe that it doesn't make any compromises in quality in comparison with regular textbooks from large publishing companies.

It's always a good idea to prepare for a course by reading the relevant chapter before the lecture. Note that there are a set of discussion questions at the end of each chapter – in general, you should be prepared to answer any of the discussion questions in class. Often, discussion questions in this book revolve around topics that are covered in Basic Marketing, or in some cases, Microeconomics courses. In effect, this book provides a good review of many of the concepts you should have already studied, and helps you see exactly how these concepts apply in an increasingly networked world.

You will note that the book is divided into four general sections. In Section I we explore the background of the marketing concepts we study in this book, including some technical details as to how digital networks work, how we provide service over such networks, and the legal and ethical implications to marketers of providing such service. Along the way, we also take a look at the kinds of marketing data that are created by networked services, and how networks have changed marketing department and company internal operations.

In Section II, the book moves into digital media from the point of view of marketing communications. It is the nature of such media that they are better suited for establishing relationships as compared to older, broadcast media. Information provided by a firm online is often a form of service, service that's provided to enhance the relationship between marketer and customer. Relationships are therefore emphasized in Section II, as are the principles by which we design these interactive services.

In Section III, we explore new digital channels of distribution. Thus, the Internet, whether it is accessed on a computer or via a mobile device, can serve a retailing function, allowing for selling online. The online channel resembles offline channels in some ways, but is unique in others. I hope you will enjoy exploring these similarities and differences. In this section, we begin looking at consumer marketing and finish by studying business marketing.

Finally, in Section IV, we contemplate new electronic services that did not exist before the Internet. In many cases, these services consist of connecting people with other people, businesses to consumers, or businesses with other businesses. For example, Facebook allows friends to connect with each other. Google allows searchers to connect with website owners and vice versa. eBay allows those who have discovered a piece of toast with a picture of their favorite college professor artistically burned into it to connect with those who might wish to buy such a thing. I'm sure there must be some buyers out there. But in the meantime, we have an interesting topic to dive into. Let's go!

Charles F. Hofacker
September 29, 2017
Tallahassee, FL

Acknowledgments

I would like to briefly thank the folks who are surely worthy of thanking. Thanks to Todd Bacile, Michael Brady, Clare Brindley, Susan Brudvig, Ashley Bush, Theresa B. Flaherty, Robert S. Moore and Jamie Murphy for their help in reviewing one or more chapters and for their suggestions. Todd, in fact, has done much more than review, as he has now provided sections of Chapters 14 and 23 as well as writing most of Chapter 25. I should emphasize that any errors are, nonetheless, my fault. I would also like to thank the Marketing Department at Florida State University for emotional, intellectual and spiritual support for many years. My chair at the time, Larry Giunipero, gave me the go-ahead to teach Internet Marketing very early on and deserves special thanks for that leap of faith. In addition, the Marketing Area at Università Bocconi deserves thanks – *grazie* – as well. Finally, a big thanks goes out to my wife Linda Vaughn for too many reasons to list here.

Section I

Marketing and digital networks

In this first section of the book we tackle a set of preliminaries. Chapter 1 starts by providing important definitions and then gives an outline of the three sections that will follow this first one: communicating, selling and connecting. Chapter 2 covers electronic service, followed by Chapter 3, a moderately technical chapter on how the Internet works. The Internet and other digital networks produce data records of the activities taking place on them. These valuable records are discussed in Chapter 4. In Chapter 5 we survey the legal and ethical challenges created by technology, technology that tends to move faster than the process of making new laws. We finish this section in Chapter 6 by investigating how digital networks change the marketing management process itself, and how these networks influence strategy and competitive advantage.

1

What is digital marketing?

Marketing has never been more challenging or more interesting. Phone companies, television, record companies and the film industry are reeling from technological disruptions to their business models. Real estate and travel agents have had to scramble in the face of changes to how consumers acquire information. The local bookstore now faces challengers that own warehouses, but no physical stores. Your local newspaper, probably dependent on revenue from classified ads, may be struggling to stay in business while sites such as eBay, Gumtree and Craigslist prosper by selling ads, and readers can get up-to-date news articles online. Today, retailers send coupons to mobile phones and customers pay for a coffee with those same phones. Firms like Facebook and Twitter did not exist a few years ago, yet today are household names with hundreds of millions of users. Google is transforming advertising, from pushing unwanted messages onto a passive audience to attracting clicks from active searchers who are actually interested in the ad. Today, Google earns far more advertising revenue than the US television network CBS and, in fact, is the largest company listed in the Fortune 500 whose revenue depends on advertising. Today, electronic games are a bigger industry than music, and revenues from gaming are on their way to surpassing the film industry. Welcome to the marketing of today and the marketing of the future. Welcome to this textbook on digital marketing.

We begin by defining a set of terms that will prove useful to us throughout this book, including the phrase "digital marketing" itself. After the section on definitions, we cover three different contexts for digital marketing. By contexts, we simply mean that there are three different situations in which we can be said to be "marketing digitally," and the three situations are sufficiently different that we need to think about which one we are in before strategizing. In fact, the entire book is organized around these three different contexts: communicating, selling and connecting. We wrap up this chapter with some historical perspective on how we got to where we are today in e-marketing. So, are you ready? Here we go. . .

Preliminary definitions

We begin with some definitions of key concepts that pertain to the subject matter of this course. To start, we turn our attention to the title of this book, digital marketing. The popular press often refers to e-commerce, but typically the word "commerce" refers to transactions. As anyone taking Basic Marketing knows, marketing goes beyond transactions. In marketing, customer relationships are considered more important than simple transactions. This book does not stop with transactions either, but deals with relationships and other customer-centered topics. Surely you know that the "e" in e-commerce refers to "electronic." In this book, I will often use the expression "electronic services," rather than digital services, out of tradition. Services marketers generally prefer the word electronic so I will honor that preference when I talk about service and services. But now, let's get back to the title of this book.

There are two words in the title: digital and marketing. Certainly, the word marketing should not cause any problems – there are lots of good definitions to fit the bill here and any one of them could be mashed together with the word digital to create a good definition of digital marketing. The word digital refers to the way that our increasingly intelligent machines store, communicate and process information. On any sort of computer, whether it is held in the hand, sits on a desktop, or is mounted in a rack in a server room, information is represented by discrete, or all-or-nothing states. These states are almost like fingers; they are either counted or not, or in other words, the state is either on or off, 1 or 0. In fact, the word digital derives from the Latin word for finger, *digitus*. The notion of the digital has come to be pervasive in our time. Even physicists believe that the universe consists of a series of all-or-nothing states.

Philosophizing aside, let's get to the definition of digital marketing:

> Digital marketing is the use of networks created from hardware and software in the process of marketing.

Digital marketing therefore happens over a network, and the network is built from both hardware and software. Networks are fairly important in the overall scheme of this book, so now let's talk about networks:

> A network is a collection of nodes, some of which are connected to other nodes.

Here the expression "node" is perfectly general and describes many different types of networks (see Chapter 22 for a more general discussion of networks). When talking about the Internet, whose full name is actually the "Internetwork," we can think of a typical node as being some sort of device, or more precisely a software program running on some device, and the connections as being effected through some combination of physical communication channels and software. All the above-mentioned software must follow certain protocols in order to successfully function as part of the Internet.

The Internet has become one of the more successful networks of all time, whether we think of success in terms of the number of nodes, the number of people who use it, or use a purely economic criterion. It started out connecting large, mainframe systems together. From there, it spread to personal computers. More recently, mobile phones, tablets and e-readers have become Internet nodes. Given this importance and ubiquity, we ought to define the Internet:

> The Internet is the sum total of devices interconnected using the Internet Protocol.

So now we have to define the Internet Protocol, often referred to as IP:

> The Internet Protocol is a set of arbitrary rules for communicating on the Internet.

I know this must sound a little circular: the Internet is the network that uses the Internet Protocol and the Internet Protocol is the protocol that is used on the Internet. In point of fact, it really is that simple. Engineers, hardware companies, software companies and users form committees and working groups that propose rules for connecting programs. Any attached device running software capable of following the rules of IP can be said to be "on" the Internet.

It is useful to understand some basic information about IP, and what it implies for the process of marketing. The IP is an open protocol, meaning that it is not controlled by any particular company. As such, it is the opposite of a proprietary protocol.

The Internet is also an open network. This means that anyone can attach anything to the Internet. The only requirement is that the attached device speaks IP, otherwise the device will not be able to communicate with any other device. The openness of the Internet, and other related design principles discussed in Chapter 3, go a long way towards explaining why IP has supplanted all previous computer communication technologies and has become the dominant way that phones are connected. Increasingly, radio is webcast rather than broadcast.

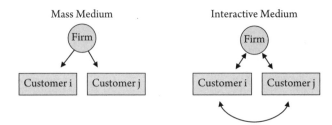

Figure 1.1 Mass media broadcast while interactive media allow for more complex communications. After Hoffman and Novak (1996)

We can also say that the Internet acts as an interactive medium. Differences between an interactive medium and a mass medium are illustrated in Figure 1.1, with an interactive medium having more complex patterns of communication, illustrated with double arrows. Communication from a firm via traditional television or radio, for example, works in a single direction only and users cannot communicate among themselves. Like the telephone network, the Internet is also a user-driven network. This might imply that it tends to work best as a pull medium rather than a push medium. Another way to express pull versus push is to think in terms of inbound marketing versus outbound marketing. A company's home page, its toll-free or free-phone number and search advertising are examples of inbound marketing, while email, Short Message Service (SMS) and banner advertisements are examples of outbound marketing.

Three contexts for digital marketing

Since the Internet, like other electronic networks, is largely "built" from software, this means that it can be made to do almost anything. We might describe it as almost chameleon-like in that regard. We can think of it as a communications medium or we can think of it as a distribution channel. In addition, there is a third way to think about it. Since the Internet is a network, that means it is ideal for connecting businesses to consumers (B2C), businesses to businesses (B2B), but also consumers to consumers (C2C). The ease with which the net creates complex connections, including C2C connections, again makes the Internet different than mass media like TV or radio.

The first context is communication, and highlights the interactivity of digital networks. When we think of the Internet as a communications medium, we can make some kind of analogy with the advertising that is done on other media. However, the existence of more complex, interactive communication possibilities online as compared to television and the mass media means that the Internet is ideal for establishing and enhancing relationships between us and our customers. And, as discussed in Chapter 2 and other chapters, we can go beyond communication and also use the Internet to perform various supplementary services for our customers. So, while the first context for the book is communication, software not only communicates, it can also act on the world and thereby provide service to and help for customers.

The second context is selling, and highlights the addressability of digital networks. Addressability refers to the fact that the digital distribution channel is direct and the selling function is not mediated by other channel partners, as is typically the case with offline retail. When we think of the Internet as a direct marketing channel, we might consider example websites where there is a physical good involved, like Amazon that ships books and other goods. We can also consider examples where the good or service being sold is purely digital, making it an information product. To illustrate, AVG provides virus protection for computers. You can buy all of AVG's products directly online and they are "shipped" to your computer over the Internet. In both the Amazon and AVG cases, software is being used to provide the traditional services offered by offline retail.

The third context is connecting, and thereby highlights the connectivity of digital networks. Digital networks allow us to create entirely new categories of business. The network along with software can be used to create platforms that allow different users to connect to each other. There are platforms that connect buyers and sellers (eBay, B2B hubs), there are platforms that connect email users and advertisers (Yahoo! Mail) and there are platforms that connect employers and job seekers (Monster.com). We can connect friends, and also advertisers (Facebook). There are lots of examples of sites that connect readers, writers and advertisers (Blogspot.com, Slate).

History of the Internet

Box 1.1 shows some key years in the development of one important electronic network used in marketing – the Internet. Many of the dates in this table are taken from the Hobbes Internet Timeline (2018).

An interesting historical side note on the development of digital networks is the role played by Xerox's Palo Alto Research Center, known as PARC. Researchers there invented many of the key technologies used by Internet adopters, including the graphical user interface, the mouse, and Ethernet. Unfortunately for Xerox it did not commercialize these inventions. The look and feel of the computer-based graphical user interface originally developed by Xerox is becoming more prevalent on a variety of devices and has changed how television programs look and feel as well.

BOX 1.1

A TIMELINE FOR DIGITAL MARKETING HISTORY

1945	Vannevar Bush contemplates the idea of linked documents
1965	Ted Nelson coins the expression hypertext
1965	The Pentagon's Defense Advanced Research Projects Agency (DARPA) studies cooperative networks
1969	First packetized message sent. It travels from the University of California, Los Angeles (UCLA) to Stanford
1970s	Net adopted by Computer Science departments at large US universities
1973	Bob Metcalfe writes his thesis on Ethernet
1977	The Apple II personal computer series is introduced
1984	Apple's HyperCard program is introduced
1986	The National Science Foundation (NSF) takes over from DARPA
1988	The NSF begins to privatize the Internet
1980s	The Net spreads to Computer Science departments worldwide
1989	Tim Berners-Lee proposes the Hypertext Transfer Protocol (HTTP)
Early 1990s	Net adopted by many non-technical academic departments
1993	The Mosaic Web browser (Firefox) is written by Marc Andreessen
1995	The NSF privatizes the Internet backbone
Late 1990s	Mass worldwide adoption of the Internet grows
Late 1990–2001	The Internet speculative financial bubble grows and bursts
2000–present	Many social networking sites garner huge success

We finish this chapter with a quote from economist George Gilder, who may have been thinking about the differences between mass and interactive media when he proclaimed in 1994 that:

> [t]he computer industry is converging with the television industry in the same sense that the automobile converged with the horse.

 QUESTIONS AND EXERCISES

1 What is your preferred definition of marketing?
2 Review the definition of a network. Give examples of networks other than the Internet.
3 What is a protocol? In what sense or senses is a protocol arbitrary?
4 In this chapter, it is claimed that the Internet works best as a pull medium rather than a push medium. Do you agree that inbound marketing is triumphing over outbound marketing? Justify your position.
5 Do a competitive analysis of two websites where the products or services in question are in direct competition. For example, Coke vs Pepsi, Jaguar vs Mercedes, Delta vs United Airlines, Hilton vs Marriott, Eveready vs Duracell, Gatorade vs Lucozade, FedEx vs UPS, or any other pair of competitors you can think of.

6 Reread the quote from George Gilder that ends this chapter. Is there any evidence that Gilder was or is correct? Do you agree with him?

 REFERENCES

Gilder, G. (1994), *Life after Television: The Coming Transformation of Media and American Life*, revised edition, New York: W.W. Norton, p. 189.

Hobbes' Internet Timeline v25 (2018), accessed January 8, 2018 at http://www.zakon.org/robert/internet/timeline/.

Hoffman, Donna L. and Thomas P. Novak (1996), "Marketing in hypermedia computer-mediated environments: Conceptual foundations," *Journal of Marketing*, **60** (3), 50–68.

2

Electronic service

An interesting way to look at the influence of technology is to realize that the
Internet is just "one big service."
(Zeithaml, Bitner and Gremler, 2006, p. 18)

The above quote should give you a sense of how important the concept of
service is in the online environment. By definition, what happens online is
a service delivered. It is no surprise then that this chapter on service will
provide a number of key concepts that will be used in much of the rest of the
book.

This chapter begins by providing some background on why much of what
happens online can in fact be considered an electronic service. After that is a
section on how we can retain users of our electronic services, a topic known
as "repatronage." Next, we discuss what happens when there is a service failure, which is unfortunately an unavoidable part of services. We wrap up this
chapter with a discussion of how we can encourage more customers to try
new electronic services.

There are many ways to deliver service to customers. For example, we can
provide a transportation service to customers by selling cars. In that case the
delivery of the transportation service occurs indirectly. We first provide a
tangible good – that is, the car – and then the car delivers the service. In other
cases, we deliver service more directly by applying our skills as a firm. Classic
examples of direct service delivery include very large parts of all advanced
economies such as entertainment, recreation, legal, business services, bank-
ing and finance, employment, insurance, hospitality, auto repair and health
care. As compared to the indirect service delivery of a tangible good, the
above sectors of the economy involve some process or act that is directly performed on behalf of the customer (Zeithaml, Parasuraman and Berry, 1985).

The Internet is a third way of delivering service. Rather than describe it as
a direct or indirect way to deliver service, we might say that it is mediated
by software. As is the case in many services, the customer helps us to create

value, a notion captured in the expression "self-service." A website is a good example of a self-service technology (SST) but apps can function as SSTs as well. Astute firms are constantly looking for ways in which the firm and the client can co-create value or otherwise increase consumer engagement, and an SST is one way to achieve those goals. In order to understand marketing on the Internet, we need to understand services, how they are co-created and consumed by our customers, and how or why those customers decide whether to stay with us, or whether to leave.

Intention to repatronize a service

It is clear that future revenue from a customer is critically important for marketers. In order to achieve any future revenue, the consumer has to want to use our service again – repatronize our service. The intention to use a service again depends on the value a consumer perceives as having resulted from the marketing exchange. This perceived value is a calculation made by the customer with respect to the costs and benefits resulting from the exchange. Following Zeithaml (1988), we can use the expressions "gives" and "gets" to represent costs and benefits. The costs do not necessarily have to be monetary in nature; they can include time costs, as well as physical and mental effort. When we describe benefits, we often think in terms of the quality with which those promised benefits are delivered. The specific benefits that attract a user to a site will depend on the purpose of that site: communicating, selling or connecting, corresponding to Sections II, III and IV of this book.

We have just noted that the intention to repurchase a service depends on the value of that service. The perceived value is a cognitive or thinking-based outcome of the service performance, but there is also an affective or emotional outcome. After the marketing exchange, the customer tends to make a comparison between the outcome he or she expected to receive and the actual outcome. The result is an emotional response known as satisfaction (or, of course, dissatisfaction), which depends on the difference between the perceived service and the expected service. If the actual performance matches or exceeds expectations, the result is satisfaction. Conversely, if the consumer's expectations are not confirmed, dissatisfaction is the result.

So, in summary, value depends on "gives" versus "gets," and satisfaction depends on expectation versus performance. In turn, value and satisfaction both combine to produce an intention to repurchase on the part of a consumer (Cronin, Brady and Hult, 2000). Figure 2.1 is a summary of Cronin et al.'s (2000) model.

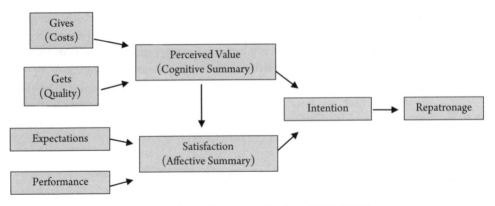

Figure 2.1 How repatronage takes place. After Cronin, Brady and Hult (2000)

Service failure

Errors in online services are almost inevitable. Online service failures occur quite frequently, either as a result of poor website design, or a temporary technical problem that leads to the site being down. Either of these cases are cause for concern for online marketers. Your website or your mobile application is like live TV; it is always being broadcast somewhere. Every second that it doesn't work is an embarrassment. The show must go on! Make sure your site always has correct information, always works, and always works well.

When errors in service delivery do occur, the marketer needs to think in terms of service recovery. Generally speaking, recovery depends on whether the error is reversible, and who is to blame for it. Assigning blame can be tricky, especially with a self-service technology, since a big part of the service performance is being executed by the customer themselves. But will the customer blame themselves or us, if things go wrong? Typical SST problems revolve around technical failure, process failure, poor design or sometimes, as has been mentioned, customer-driven failure. Conversely, when the consumer's expectations of an SST are exceeded this can generate sheer delight.

Components of e-service

We can distinguish different components of a service offering, as have Van Riel, Liljander and Jurriens (2001). These authors distinguish between the core service and a supplementary service. The performance of the core service generates the core benefits of the offering. The core benefit of a retailing website is that it allows you to buy things on it. In this case, the core benefit of retailing has been transformed to the online channel. This is the subject of Section III, which deals with selling. There are also some online services that do not or could not exist offline. For example, Google offers the core service of connecting searchers with those who wish to be found. The core service of making connections is the topic of the very last section of the book, Section IV.

A supplementary service can be a facilitating service that is mandatory for consumption, like a ticket. On the other hand, a supporting service is a type of supplementary service that is not mandatory but rather is used to differentiate the offering, like high-quality popcorn at an upscale movie theater. We see many different types of supplementary services online. Piccoli et al. (2004) have listed the following examples:

- hospitality and welcoming;
- consulting and advice;
- exception handling;
- new goods and services;
- order taking;
- billing and payment; and
- caretaking and safekeeping.

Frequently, firms that sell offline or provide an offline service will use the online medium to provide a supporting service. For example, FedEx transports packages for clients, and its website and mobile servers allow clients to track their packages. Department stores sell offline but they allow brides-to-be to register online and friends can find out on the Internet what the couple would like in the way of wedding gifts. Your town's Parks and Recreation department might provide offline soccer fields for residents but it might also let you see on its website if a particular field is free on a particular night.

Adoption of technology by consumers

To succeed with a new self-service technology, a firm has to hope that consumers will stop using the service the old way, and adopt the new approach. What factors determine whether consumers will adopt a new self-service technology? There are two types: characteristics of the innovation and characteristics of the consumer (Meuter et al., 2005).

Let's start by thinking about what characteristics of the innovation are conducive to rapid adoption. For one thing, to the extent that the new self-service is compatible with the old service, relatively simple or easy to use, with minimal risk, the consumer will take to it quickly. Likewise, if the new approach is obviously highly useful and has a clear relative advantage over the old and that advantage is very observable, there will be a quick adoption process. Another key factor is the trialability of the self-service technology. Can the technology be tried in small steps or is it a big, all-or-nothing move to switch to the new one?

Now let's think about the characteristics of the consumer. Some consumers exhibit behavioral inertia. In other words, some of us don't really like to change how we do things. Adding to problems associated with inertia is technological anxiety, or to use another phrase, computer phobia. No doubt you know some people who are afflicted with that! In addition, some of us like to interact with our fellow human beings (called sociality) while some of us would generally prefer to not have to deal with people. Of course, experience with technology and simple demographics can make a difference as well. For these and more reasons, some consumers are readier for new technology than others. To be ready, we normally have to be clear on the role we are going to play in the SST, we need to be motivated, and we need to have the ability or skill to successfully interact with the SST (Meuter et al., 2005).

 QUESTIONS AND EXERCISES

1 It has been claimed (Zeithaml et al., 1985) that services tend to be less tangible than physical goods. Thus, an insurance policy, which is a financial service, is intangible. Let's consider a supplementary online service, such as when FedEx allows customers to enter the tracking number of a package on its website. In your opinion, is this supplementary service intangible?

2 It has also been claimed that services tend to be more heterogeneous than tangible goods. The haircut I receive may vary depending on the mood or concentration of the stylist. Let's consider iTunes. In your opinion, is the core service of buying a song from iTunes heterogeneous?

3 It has been further claimed that for most services, the service provider and the service client need to be together at the same place at the same time for the service performance. Thus, most services are inseparable – to get my hair cut, the stylist and I have to be in the same room at the same time. Let's consider Google. In your opinion, if I use Google to find a doctor in my home town, is that core service provided by Google inseparable?

4 Finally, it has been claimed that most services cannot be inventoried, but disappear, in effect, once the performance is over. Here we need only to think about an empty seat on an airline. Once the plane takes off, the service offering is, as the French say, *fait accompli*. That seat is perishable. Let's consider iTunes again. Is the core service of buying and downloading songs perishable?

5 As described in this chapter, the characteristics of an e-services innovation can determine the speed with which consumers adopt that innovation. As compared with the old way of doing things, what are the characteristics of using an e-reader for a textbook instead of paper? Now consider online matchmaking services like eHarmony. As a final example, suppose a fleet of self-driving cars were available in your town that could be summoned via an app when you needed a ride. Can we predict the speed of adoption for these services based on the properties of the innovations?

6 What is behind the trend towards self-service? Many countries are increasingly experiencing non-Internet examples, such as ATM machines, grocery self-bagging, kiosks for ticket purchase, automated telephone menus, pump your own gas, and so on. As a consumer, do you like this trend? How does the trend impact competition among firms?

REFERENCES

Cronin, J.J., M.K. Brady and G.T.M. Hult (2000), "Assessing the effects of quality, value, and customer satisfaction on consumer behavioral intentions in service environments," *Journal of Retailing*, **76** (2), 193–218.

Meuter, M.L., M.J. Bitner, A.L. Ostrom and S.W. Brown (2005), "Choosing among alternative service delivery modes: An investigation of customer trial of self-service technologies," *Journal of Marketing*, **69** (2), 61–83.

Piccoli, G., M.K. Brohman, R.T. Watson and A. Parasuraman (2004), "Net-based customer service systems: Evolution and revolution in website functionalities," *Decision Sciences*, **35** (3), 423–55.

Van Riel, A.C.R., V. Liljander and P. Jurriens (2001), "Exploring consumer evaluations of e-services: A portal site," *International Journal of Service Industry Management*, **12** (4), 359–77.

Zeithaml, V.A. (1988), "Consumer perceptions of price, quality, and value: A means-end model and synthesis of evidence," *Journal of Marketing*, **52** (3), 2–22.

Zeithaml, V.A., M.J. Bitner and D.D. Gremler (2006), *Services Marketing*, fourth edition, Boston, MA: McGraw-Hill/Irwin.

Zeithaml, V.A., A. Parasuraman and L.L. Berry (1985), "Problems and strategies in services marketing," *Journal of Marketing*, **49** (2), 33–46.

3

Internet design and philosophy

Each medium has its own properties, and its properties condition the ways that people adapt to a medium, use it, and derive benefits from it. Chapter 1 claims that the Internet is unlike the mass media; that in fact it is a user-driven interactive medium. So, what does this mean? The philosophy underlying the Internet provides important clues to how marketing must adapt to that medium. These clues come in the form of three key philosophical principles from information systems design.

First, there is the end-to-end principle. According to this philosophy (Saltzer, Reed and Clark, 1984), processing should occur at the ends of the communication process, which is to say, as close as possible to the resource being utilized. This principle leads to the odd notion that the Internet was designed as a dumb network. The intelligence in the Internet is located at the periphery of the network, on user desktops, in user pockets, and in the servers.

The principle implies that the network or the server should not perform any action that can be done at the user's end of the network instead. For example, unlike magazine ads that we format to the hundredth of an inch, the Hypertext Transfer Protocol (HTTP) allows text to flow into the space allotted to it on the user's window. We may think our company page looks good on our browser, but the user is in control of the size of the window and the fonts in use. We need to honor this power on the part of the user and not try to insist on controlling everything. More than with magazines or other mass media, the user co-produces his or her Internet service. As users gain access to ever more powerful computers, it makes sense that those computers are being called upon to play a greater role in the communication process. The user, after all, is sitting in front of a computer that a few decades ago would be considered a supercomputer. Online, the consumer and the marketer play roles that are closer to being equal, at least when compared to their traditional offline roles. The user controls his or her online experience to a much greater degree than with the mass media.

The second principle is modularity. Modularity is a design philosophy that allows for blissful ignorance on the part of programmers. Modularity suggests that we keep interdependence low across modules, and it allows for module communication rules, so that each programmer can worry about creating or adding cool services and not have to spend an overly long amount of time coordinating with all the other programmers working on other modules.

Third, the Internet roughly follows the Open Systems Interconnection (OSI) model. This is a way of using layers to apply both the end-to-end and modularity principles. Each layer is built on top of the previous layer, and is modular with respect to lower layers. There are seven "layers" in this system, in ascending order:

1. physical layer;
2. data link layer;
3. network layer;
4. transport layer;
5. session layer;
6. presentation layer;
7. application layer.

As has been mentioned, each of these layers is built on top of the previous layer, and programmers working on one layer do not have to worry about what is happening at lower layers (an example of modularity). The very lowest layers are closest to the hardware and the higher levels are closer to the user. We take a brief tour of all seven layers. We start our tour at the bottom – at the physical layer.

Physical layer

The physical layer translates bits into physical signals and vice versa. In other words, it sends and receives 1s and 0s using radio waves, wires or strands of glass fiber. The physical layer is in charge of dealing with the specific transmission medium, which might take the form of Category 5 twisted pair, fiber, coaxial, Wi-Fi or infrared. The kind of equipment operating here includes network gear such as the Network Interface Card (NIC), repeaters and hubs.

Data link layer

Data are linked to and from the physical device and communication errors are corrected at this layer. The network gear that operates at this level includes switches and bridges. This gear is often used to create a local area network or LAN, or sometimes a wide area network (WAN).

Ethernet is one of the key standards that exists at this layer. I am going to briefly describe Ethernet because it epitomizes the technology design philosophy that relies on inexpensive but powerful processors operating at the edge of the network (as opposed to a hypothetical center of the network). Imagine a conversation where no one bothered to notice if anyone else in the conversation was talking at the same time, but everybody was smart enough to listen to hundreds of conversations at the same time so it didn't matter. In the same way, an Ethernet broadcasts, rather than coordinates, network data traffic. As such, it is a typical geek way of solving the problem – throw cheap chips at it! Why bother to carefully coordinate data coming and going on a network? If two packets collide, just send them again. The chips are so fast that no one will even notice.

An Ethernet device like an NIC utilizes a Media Access Control (MAC) address. These addresses always appear in the form of six base 16 numbers, for example 00-a0-33-0f-dd-8c. These cards sift through the anarchy of packets flying by them on a LAN and simply throw away all the packets not addressed to them. Here we have a sort of parable for the way that the Internet works. In the online environment, no one dares to assert control. Instead, anarchy reigns, but the silicon, the chips on the user's machine, sort it all out and make it work.

The service experience on a network depends greatly on the data link layer. If I am accessing the network via an overloaded mobile cell tower in San Francisco, my service experience at your website may be completely different than someone sitting in Seoul who has a very-high-bit-rate digital subscriber line (VDSL) modem operating at 100 000 000 bits per second.

Network layer

This is where the Internet Protocol (IP), as described in Chapter 1, operates. IP handles routing and forwarding. Its basic job is to create or simulate a "virtual" network; thus, it allows for the connection of dissimilar LANs. The existence and adoption of IP has greatly reduced business costs for using network technology. All the hardware vendors were forced, for competitive reasons, to support IP in the 1990s. This shifted the balance of power in favor of companies buying network gear as opposed to those who were selling it. The ascendancy of the business customer in this exchange forced the hardware vendors into competing on price rather than trying to lock customers into proprietary network technology. As for consumers, the degree of IP's triumph in the marketplace has made decision making easy. If a computer or software program is not compatible with the Internet, the consumer does not even bother to consider it. The investment needed to connect to the Internet is modest while the benefits are high. Thus, the consumer perceives high value.

IP deals with packets of data. All IP traffic, whether it be web pages, email or videos, is broken into data packets that make their way from the sender to the receiver separately and are recombined by the receiver's device in real time. Network devices known as routers blindly forward these packets from the sender in the general direction of the receiver. Each router gets the packets a step closer and they "eventually" arrive on the receiver's machine and are put in the correct order. Even Internet phone calls and videos work this way. It is here that the essential dumbness of the Internet is on display. The network itself merely forwards packets. The intelligence is at the periphery – or the "end" – where plenty of horsepower is available to provide a seamless service experience. Much of this computing horsepower is contributed by the user's machine. The end-to-end principle in effect is an endorsement of the services marketing philosophy that the consumer co-creates value along with the firm. Network services tend to be co-produced services, right down to the network layer. This is built into the philosophy of the Internet.

All devices on the Internet have an address, known as an IP address. These have traditionally looked like four decimal (base 10) numbers separated by dots: 128.186.6.1, otherwise known as a dotted quad. The newer version of IP (Version 6, or Internet Protocol next generation) allows for eight four-digit hexadecimal (base 16) numbers separated by colons, as in 8BC3:EF44: 84AC:CA77:238E:8272:BB02:0000. IP addresses are translated into human languages by the Domain Name Service (DNS), which we discuss when we reach the application layer.

Transport layer

The transport layer is charged with taking data in and out of packets. It provides end-to-end control and error checking. The key protocol here is called Transmission Control Protocol (TCP). This layer is the one that allows any set of computers to communicate with each other.

Session layer

The session layer establishes communication sessions, coordinates sessions, transfers data, deals with session security and releases sessions. It is based on numbered logical ports. For example, the HTTP traditionally uses logical port 80 to create brief sessions in which a server sends a page.

Presentation layer

The presentation layer is a syntax layer that interprets bit streams for users. It deals with graphics, audio, text, video, some encryption protocols, and performs compression and packing and unpacking. It is typically part of the operating system (i.e., for most of us, Windows, iOS or Android). The protocols you might have heard of that operate at the presentation level include MIME, ASCII, jpeg, mpeg and gif.

Application layer

This is the part that we users see and that deals with files, printing, data, web pages, videos, pictures and so forth. There are a lot of different applications on digital networks, and developers are always inventing new ones. There is chat, instant messaging, BitTorrent, Flash, RealAudio, RSS feeds, numerous Facebook applications, and on and on. For our purposes, we limit ourselves in this chapter to discussing five of them: the World Wide Web, social, email, messaging and the Domain Name Service.

The World Wide Web (WWW)

This is a network application that operates according to a client–server model. In a client–server model, there are two different roles played by two different pieces of software. The server waits for requests and sends out information. The client, on the other hand, requests information and acts at the end of the communication chain to present that information to the user based on local conditions such as window size and user preferences. The Web client is typically called a browser. The Web utilizes a stateless connection, which is to say that no permanent connection is established between the server and the browser. Over the years, the Web has expanded to include text, audio, graphics of various sorts and video. It also has an input capability. In general, the WWW represents a fairly low barrier to entry. Thus, even small firms have some sort of Web presence.

One could argue that the website is still the focal point of digital marketing. Websites give businesses a huge potential numeric and geographic reach. The Web allows even small firms to establish a presence online and to leverage offline ads. As discussed in Chapter 2, the Web is clearly in line with the move to a self-service philosophy. The Web can be made to perform either an advertising or retail function, or it can be used to help customers connect to each other. Unlike mass media, web pages can be easily changed or updated.

Social

Social media include services such as Facebook, LinkedIn and Twitter but sites where content is contributed and shared by individuals (discussed in Chapter 23) and their friends like YouTube, Pinterest and Flickr have a social component. If the World Wide Web is a network where the nodes are documents, social media create networks where the nodes are people. Of course, Facebook and the other examples I have just given can be accessed as websites, thus blurring the distinction between these sorts of applications. Facebook and its competitors were built using Web client–server protocols and later expanded into mobile. Social media are discussed further in Chapter 25.

Email

Classic email, which we all know and love, operates according to a "store and forward" mechanism. It is thus an asynchronous communication medium. Asynchronous simply means that the communicating parties do not need to be connected at the same time. Email tends to be long lasting and it operates at a mid-level of formality and of urgency. Email also has great flexibility in terms of who receives it. Having added pictures and other Web-like characteristics, email has become a richer medium.

Once prepared, the marginal cost of adding one additional email recipient is very low or zero (see Figure 3.1). The low marginal cost of digital communication and electronic services has many implications for marketing, especially for pricing. These implications are addressed in Chapter 22.

Figure 3.1 The cost to send an email, versus postal mail, based on how many people are to receive it

At this point, we might understand why spam is so prevalent. An estimate by Kanich et al. (2008) suggests that email is so cheap that purchase rates from spam as low as 0.0000081 percent might still be profitable! No one, not even a scam artist, has problems in affording the price of getting email messages out. The problem for legitimate marketers is one of attracting the attention of the overwhelmed consumer. Attention is discussed at length in Chapter 10.

One key enabling protocol for email is known as Simple Mail Transfer Protocol (SMTP). This operates from the client to server and from server to server. Traditionally, users had dedicated, specialized clients to access email including Outlook, Outlook Express, Lotus, Eudora and Thunderbird. More recently, the Web browser has been adapted to serve as an email client, with services such as Hotmail, Yahoo! Mail, and Gmail all becoming more popular.

Email can be somewhat dangerous to use to communicate with clients. Be aware that it is hard to express attitude or mood using plain text so that email can be easily misinterpreted. Also, do not confuse email with SMS texting. The former is much more formal, and can easily be copied and distributed with potentially embarrassing results. This means that good grammar and spelling should be maintained on all company-related emails to convey a professional image.

Messaging

There are several different messaging protocols in use today including SMS, Facebook Messenger, Skype's service that allows you to type instead of or in addition to using voice, WhatsApp, and many others. Once again these applications blur the lines; software is flexible and tends to be slippery when we want to define things exactly! SMS is mostly used on mobile platforms but can also be used on the Web via Google Voice and other means. Twitter can be used to broadcast SMS messages to many people at once, although some of them might receive those messages on their desktop machines. Likewise, a Facebook message can be sent or received on a computer or on a smartphone. SMS is asynchronous like email, but some messaging services, usually called as "chat," require that all communicating parties be connected simultaneously.

These applications, the Web, social, email and messaging, create a variety of touch points between the firm and its customers. To that list we could add mobile and classic offline face-to-face. The multiplicity of channels poses two dilemmas for marketers. One dilemma revolves around the amount of money to invest in each channel. Second, if I get a sale, to which touch point should I attribute that sale? In other words, which touch point gets the credit? This second dilemma is hard to resolve since customers often use more than one channel in their interactions with the company. We now turn to the final application of the chapter, DNS. DNS in some sense is a metaphor for the decentralized nature of the Internet Protocol.

Domain Name Service

The Domain Name Service, or DNS, translates between site names, like www.fsu.edu (Florida State University), and physical network addresses, like 192.168.1.1 (see the above discussion on IP addresses). DNS provides a great example of what modularity means in practice. There is no server on the Internet that knows, or could know, all the IP addresses on the network. A solution based on a central server with a big address table would not scale. Here "scale" is used as a verb and means a solution that will continue to work as you go from 10 to 100 to trillions of addresses.

Instead, the DNS system is completely decentralized, and the knowledge of what domain name goes with what IP address is left to local servers. If someone wants to look at www.fsu.edu, their DNS server will query a so-called root server. The root server will not know the answer, but it will know the address of the DNS server that knows about .edu addresses. The .edu server will not know the answer either, but it will know the address of the server that specializes in the fsu.edu domain. That machine, which is based on the FSU campus and is called dns.fsu.edu, is charged with knowing the address of www.fsu.edu and other campus machines. All businesses and universities that have their own domain rely on DNS in a similar manner.

The Domain Name Service offers us another parable of the Internet design philosophy and how that impacts marketing. A company's domain name is an extension of its brand, its identity. On the Internet, the naming process is highly decentralized, with each module running on a different DNS server responsible for a small piece of the universe of Internet names, also called the Internet name space. This leads to inevitable conflict between parties wishing to leverage the same name. These conflicts, and the legal clashes they have engendered, are the topic of Chapter 5.

While numerous new applications are being built every day, the above list of five should give you a feel for what the application layer does and how it impacts users on the Internet and other digital networks. If you have a Facebook account, you have no doubt seen the variety and number of applications running on just that platform, including multiplayer games and sharing applications. Likewise, if you use a tablet or smartphone, there are numerous types of applications to try. Since application services are built from software, they can be made to do almost anything. This flexibility implies that the most important aspects of designing new online services are human thoughts, feelings and behaviors. The rest we can work out with software code. Flexibility is built into the Internet by virtue of the OSI model. The end-to-end principle, and its insistence on minimal network standards, implies that we should honor the power that the consumer has on his or her desktop. Online, the user co-produces his or her service experience to a large degree.

Taken together, the principles discussed in this chapter explain why digital entrepreneurs can achieve scale so quickly. Well-made software is scalable, meaning that a new company can go from a thousand to a million to a billion customers faster than at any time in history. The digital world does not grow linearly; it tends to move by adding zeros (10, 100, 1000. . .), which is to say exponentially.

 QUESTIONS AND EXERCISES

1 It has been said that the Web does not create an entry barrier for firms.
    (a) What does the expression entry barrier mean?
    (b) What is the implication of low entry barriers for competition?
    (c) Do you think it is true that the Web does not have entry barriers?
2 Compare how applications are created for the Internet, with the design philosophy used there, with how apps are created for the Apple iPad.
3 Many larger companies are multidivisional corporations, owning numerous brand names. Some salient examples are Kraft Foods (Gevalia, Philadelphia Cream Cheese, Planter's Nuts) or General Motors (Chevrolet, Buick, Cadillac). Should these companies have a single domain name and each brand is a page under that name, or should each brand have its own domain name? Why would you strategize the way you suggest?
4 A recent trend, known as cloud computing, removes responsibility from the user's hardware and gives more responsibility to the server. A good example of this trend is Google Docs, which allows users to do word processing even if they do not have any word processing software. The document is stored on the server and is ideal for collaborating and sharing work across multiple authors. Does cloud computing go against the end-to-end principle?
5 In this assignment, pick four brands that you, or a family member, have recently purchased. These could be any consumer good or service: a car, a haircut, a restaurant meal, a frozen dinner from a supermarket, a pair of shoes, jewelry, a ticket to a concert, a medical appointment, clothing, electronics, a household appliance, a replacement battery or light bulb, anything. Guess the website name for this product. Do not use Google or any other search engine! The idea is to guess. For each of your chosen four purchases, write down what you saw when you typed in the address corresponding to your best guess for each product. Was it what you expected, or did some other company own the name?
6 Is the website still the focal point of digital marketing? Will mobile or social become the new

central focus of digital marketing? If you think the Web still rules, for how long will it rule? What challenges will Web-focused firms face?

 REFERENCES

Kanich, C., C. Kreibich and K. Levchenko et al. (2008), "Spamalytics: An empirical analysis of spam marketing conversion," in *Proceedings of the 15th ACM Conference on Computer and Communications Security*, Alexandria, VA: Association for Computing Machinery.

Saltzer, J.H., D.P. Reed and D.D. Clark (1984), "End-to-end arguments in system design," *ACM Transactions on Computer Systems*, **2** (4), 277–88.

4

Observational and experimental data

When a company spends money on advertising in the mass media, it is an act of faith that the advertisement is actually seen or heard by anyone. With television, the signal shoots through the air or across some cables into somebody's living room. But, of course, we don't know what is going on in that living room. Is anyone in there? Are they paying attention? The company can learn what happened to its message only by paying for expensive research. Likewise, when a manufacturer produces a box of cereal, sells it to a retailer and the retailer in turn sells it to the consumer, the manufacturer is basically cut out of the picture. Who bought it? When did they buy it? The manufacturer can learn these facts only by pleading with, and most likely paying, the retailer or by performing expensive research.

The Internet, on the other hand, is a direct channel between the firm and the customer. Whatever communication or financial exchange occurs, the firm knows about it if it takes the time to look at the data. Digital networks tend to be addressable (Blattberg and Deighton, 1991), meaning that we know who receives the message. This makes media like the Web and mobile more accountable than a mass medium, and more direct than traditional retail. Given this accountability and directness, the smart marketer will study and learn from data.

While all digital processes throw off data, not all of it will be accessible to the firm. Nevertheless, log data are created by the company's own servers, so this is always available. Likewise, if the firm has implemented e-commerce software, this will capture sales data and ideally store customer data in a form that allows the firm to assess its relationship with that customer (see Chapter 7). Mobile apps can be programmed to save data, so you know when someone uses your app. On the other hand, clickstream data (described later in this chapter) have to be purchased, and advertising response data (Chapter 14 and also mentioned below) are owned by whoever controls the advertising network platform. Since log data are freely available and fairly simple, these will be described below as a good example.

What are log data?

Every time you request a document using the Web, the server sends it to you, but then it takes one extra action – it writes a record to a log file. A log record includes the following:

- **The Internet Protocol (IP) address of the client:** If the server is so configured, the domain name of the client will also be logged. If not, the domain name can be looked up after the fact.
- **The date and time:** The exact time and date is "stamped" into the log file.
- **The file name requested:** What did the client want?
- **The return code:** This is a three-digit number summarizing the result of the request. You have probably seen at least one of these. . .the infamous "404" error. This is the return code generated when the page was not found. If everything goes well, the code is 200.
- **The number of bytes transferred:** How much stuff was sent in the client's direction is logged.
- **The referrer page:** This is the Uniform Resource Locator (URL or web address) that the client was on when they made the current request. This allows you to see one page back in the navigation sequence of the client, even when that page is not on your site. For example, if they came from Google, you can see the keywords the client entered into Google before clicking on your page since that is built into the URL that Google creates for results pages.
- **The specific client software requesting the page:** You can see whether they are using Internet Explorer, Firefox, Opera, Chrome or some other browser. You can also see the client version.

The good news from all these data is that we know a lot about the consumer's hardware and software. The bad news is that we do not know much about the consumer themselves.

We can, of course, learn more about the consumer by asking them to register or log on to our site. If registration is required, we can analyze any variable that we require for registration. In addition, we can connect the current visit with previous visits. For a communications site this might include the contact history, while for a selling site this might include the purchase history. But registration obviously slows down the visitor and might cause them to balk at our request or worse yet, leave our site. On the other hand, tracking the history of the relationship between your firm and a specific client is incredibly useful and valuable. Relationship data are covered in detail in Chapter 7. Often firms supplement their own data using list brokers. These are firms that buy and aggregate consumer data.

Registered or not, every time a client requests a page, we see another log record as described above. So, if a client retrieves a second page from us a few minutes later, unless they got up and changed computers, their IP address will tend to be the same. This allows us to make a reasonable inference about the client's site visit, or visit for short. We might define a visit as a series of log records coming from the same IP address, where the time elapsed between any two log records is less than 30 minutes (Novak and Hoffman, 1997).

If we want to remember what happened on previous visits, we can use the Hypertext Transfer Protocol (HTTP) to set a cookie on the visitor's hard drive. A cookie is a small file that the server can write on the user's machine. The next time the user returns to the site, the cookie can be read back. Cookies are also indispensable to retargeting or remarketing. Retargeting occurs when a retail company places a cookie on a user's computer during a visit, and that user, in the course of his or her Internet navigation, eventually arrives at some other site that belongs to the same ad network as the retailer. The retailer then pays for a banner ad that beckons the user back to the retailer's site. Online marketers believe that retargeting represents a very effective use of advertising expenditures. Despite its effectiveness, however, cookies are not without controversy. Many consumers, and some marketers, consider them a violation of the consumer's privacy.

Observing Web behavior

There are two different ways we can use log data. First, we can simply observe the data. Let's call this passive observation. Passively looking at our log data allows us to discover the answers to many important questions. Such questions might include:

- On which page do visitors arrive?
- Where do they come from?
- What pages are most and least popular?
- What is the last page most visitors see?
- What are common navigation sequences?
- What sorts of mistakes do people make?
- What search terms are site visitors using to find us?

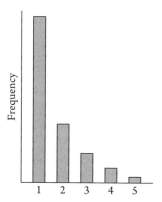

The answer to these questions can be found by looking at Web log data. They teach us about visitor navigation and inform us about how these visitors are using the site. There are also specific questions that we might ask if our goal is to establish or enhance a relationship with customers, as is the case when our website is designed primarily for communication:

● How many pages do visitors typically see?
● How much time do they spend on our site?

Figure 4.1 is a hypothetical graph of page visits. The height of the first bar is proportional to the number of visitors who saw one page, while the height of the other bars provides the number of people who saw two, three, four pages and so on.

If our site is designed around creating transactions, as would be the case for an "e-tail" site, we will be interested in a more specific Web metric:

● What is our conversion efficiency?

To explain conversion efficiency, let's think about e-tail, where our goal is for the visitor to execute a transaction, which is to say, to actually purchase something. To execute a transaction, let's imagine that the visitor must click on the product page, from there click on the purchase page, and then finally make the purchase on that page. In effect, each of those steps is like a hurdle or obstacle that must be overcome for that transaction to be executed. At each page, we lose some of our visitors but hopefully a large percentage keeps going. The conversion efficiency of each page is the percentage of visitors that go on to the next step. Likewise, if our goal is to provide a supplementary service, like appointment scheduling or shipment tracking, we might be interested in how many people are converted at each step along the way to

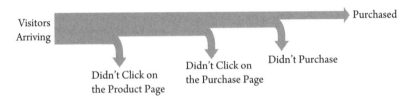

Figure 4.2 One way to graph conversion efficiency

using that service and how many drop out at each step. One way to represent conversion efficiency is given in Figure 4.2.

At each of the four steps, the conversion efficiency is the proportion of people who do not drop out of the process. A low conversion efficiency is diagnostic of a problem with the step associated with it.

Web experiments

Second, Beyond passive observation, we can also change our site and see how that affects the log data. We can call that technique active experimentation. For example, imagine that we are not sure about which of two page designs would be more effective: home page version A or home page version B. We can replace the home page with a computer program that randomly shows either A or B to each arriving visitor. The computer program then adds a record to its own log file, noting both the IP address of the visitor and which page that visitor saw. We can then look and see what happened with that visitor. How many and which links did the visitor click on? How long did they stay on the site? Did they buy anything? Did they enter any data that allow us to learn about them?

After some period of time, we pick a winner, A vs B, and that becomes our new home page until someone in our company comes up with a new idea to test. Then we pit the new design against the previous winner. We can use this basic technique at three levels of investigation: link or banner design, page design, and at the level of the structure of the whole site.

With regard to link or banner design, we might test various factors including copy, size, color, movement or graphical components. In terms of page design, we might have different versions of a page with a different number and type of links, different physical formatting, positioning of design elements or use of images. We can investigate click cannibalization in this way. In other words, we can learn if new links create additional engagement on the page, or if instead they merely take clicks away from pre-existing links.

Switching to overall site design, we can have two versions of the entire site if we want! Perhaps we alternate these – automatically of course – every half hour. We could investigate how to structure our menus, how much and where to modularize, and the use of different navigation bars.

A key difference between digital and most other forms of communication is that the digital media are dynamic. The only way to take advantage of this dynamism on the Web is to change your site! Web log data provide critical information as to how to change the site but what's more, virtually any marketing variable can be the subject of an active experiment. You can test your marketing communications, your prices, the effectiveness of sales promotions and any branding components. All that is needed are multiple versions of the pages or images in question, and the ability to switch between those versions. Switching can even be done by hand.

Experiments are ideal for quantifying cause-and-effect relationships. On the one hand, you have a set of variables called decision variables that you control, such as the format of your page. On the other hand, you have a variable that serves as a measure of success (clicks, page views, number of transactions, sales, profit). This second type of variable is the objective. The results of experiments can be used to calibrate analytical models (discussed in Chapter 7) that relate decision variables to objective functions.

For now, three examples should clarify the benefits of experimentation. Jared Spool (2009) of User Interface Engineering recounts that he changed a single button and earned a client firm an extra $300 million of revenue per year! In another example, a well-known big-box retailer in the US modified its search landing page by changing it from a list of stock keeping units (SKUs) to a "research page" and saw its sales go up by 38 percent. The same retailer added the possibility for a chat session on its site. At first, the experimenter thought that no improvement had been made since sales did not go up, but as a week went by it was realized that product returns had gone way down, more than enough to justify the expense of the live chat.

Of course, these examples just scratch the surface of what we can learn from experiments. App designers can tweak the app's appearance and function to optimize its performance in the market. Banner ads can be tested. Search keywords can be pitted against each other. Direct marketers have long known and practiced the power of experimentation. Instead of relying on "instinct" or guesswork, direct marketers at companies like Google constantly experiment, and constantly improve the service to and communication with customers. It is nearly always the case that testing beats the HiPPO – the highest-paid person's opinion (Christian, 2012).

Clickstream data

While server log data, described above, are similar to store scanner data, clickstream data resemble consumer panel data. Instead of being collected at the server, clickstream data are collected at the user level, with ordinary people recruited to participate in an online panel. Software is then installed on their machine, and the software creates a record of all the pages that individual visits. This allows marketers to understand the user's full set of online habits and choices, and gives us a good picture of what is going on when consumers search, for example. As you might imagine, clickstream data tend to be fairly expensive, but any marketer trying to understand a product category might be interested in spending the money to purchase a panel (see Du, Kamakura and Mela, 2007).

Usability data

The task of good site design is very hard. How can anyone know how consumers will use a website? Since no one can know, testing becomes extremely important. A classic way to test a website is by taking a small group of users and giving them a typical task to solve on the website. You then watch them and have them think aloud while they use your site to perform the task. You can record errors they make and note the percentage of successful task completions. If the site is too hard, go back and fix it. The ability for users to do what they want to do on a website is called the usability of the site.

? QUESTIONS AND EXERCISES

1 Web log data are a type of behavioral data. In other words, they measure how people behave. On the other hand, marketers frequently use questionnaires. What can questionnaires measure? What are the advantages and disadvantages of behavioral data as compared to questionnaire data?

2 What sort of log data will be most important:
   (a) If my site generates revenue for me by selling advertising space?
   (b) If my site is designed for selling and shipping goods to consumers?
   (c) If my site is designed to broaden engagement with a service to consumers that is sold offline?

3 What are the pros and cons of forcing website visitors to register for a website?

4 Suggest an experiment for your university's website. What aspect of the site would you test?

5 Suggest an experiment that might be run by a mobile app developer.

6 If your university was going to perform usability testing on its website, what tasks would it give students to do?

7   Do you configure your browser to block cookies on any of your computers? Why or why not?

 REFERENCES

Blattberg, R.C. and J. Deighton (1991), "Interactive marketing: Exploiting the age of addressability," *Sloan Management Review*, **33** (1), 5–14.

Christian, B. (2012), "The A/B test: Inside the technology that's changing the rules of business," *Wired*, April 25, accessed January 9, 2018 at http://www.wired.com/business/2012/04/ff_abtesting/.

Du, R.Y., W.A. Kamakura and C.F. Mela (2007), "Size and share of customer wallet," *Journal of Marketing*, **71** (2), 94–113.

Novak, T.P. and D.L. Hoffman (1997), "New metrics for new media: Toward the development of Web measurement standards," *World Wide Web Journal*, **2** (1), 213–46.

Spool, J.M. (2009), "The $300 million button," *UIE*, n.d., accessed January 9, 2018 at http://www.uie.com/articles/three_hund_million_button/.

5

Legal and ethical aspects of digital marketing

In July, 2017, the CEO of iRobot, Colin Angle, couldn't help but brag a bit about the company's Roomba 960 and Roomba 980 models. iRobot's engineers had endowed those robotic vacuum cleaners with the ability to build and communicate a detailed map of their owner's home. The CEO told Reuters that, "There's an entire ecosystem of things and services that the smart home can deliver once you have a rich map of the home that the user has allowed to be shared" (Wolf, 2017). Angle told Reuters that the company might soon make a deal to share its home mapping data with Google, Apple or Amazon. As a consumer, you may think this sharing is a cool idea, or it may creep you out. As a marketer, the one thing you cannot do is ignore the ethical or legal implications of sharing such personal data with third parties.

In recent years, major ethical scandals have rocked the world of business. Many people have been hurt by businesses' unethical behavior. Nurturing the relationship with current, former and potential customers is a fundamental basis of marketing. We cannot nurture anything by behaving unethically.

All of us can use the word ethics in a sentence, but coming up with a good definition for the word is more of a challenge. For the purpose of our class, we can define it as follows:

> Ethics is a set of principles or standards that determine whether an action is right (good) or wrong (bad) and which therefore informs us what we ought and ought not do.

Societies consider ethical behavior to be paramount, which requires that firms explicitly address ethics.

Privacy

Almost no online issue has more potential for raising ethical questions – and potentially depressing revenue – than the issue of consumer privacy. For our purposes, we will define privacy as "the right to limit access to the self." Of particular concern is information concerning our medical, sexual and financial selves, and information on where we are geographically speaking. When we speak of digital data on the customer, we therefore need to treat personally identifiable information (PII) with special care, especially if it is tied to sensitive information categories.

It is interesting to note that the European Union (EU) and the United States differ in their privacy laws. The EU, via Data Protection Directive 95/46/EC (to be superseded by the General Data Protection Regulation in May 2018), requires informed consent. This means that use of personal data by the website owner is prohibited unless site visitors explicitly opt-in. Websites in the United States, on the other hand, are required to have a policy statement somewhere on the website. US law allows the use of personal data by the website owner unless site visitors explicitly opt-out. In general, the US tends to allow industries to self-regulate more than Europe does. There is an exception to the US law, however. The Children's Online Privacy Protection Act (COPPA) requires parental consent to use of data when the age of the visitor is under 13.

In any case, it is of course appropriate to explain to customers or users why you are collecting personal information. Certainly, the consumer would seem to be justified in worrying about privacy: in July, 2017 the credit reporting agency Equifax discovered that personal information on 143 million Americans had been hacked (Lieber, 2017). The information stored by Equifax could be a huge boon to identity thieves. Consumers want a choice as to how their information is used and they would like to be able to review their information and its use, to correct it if it is wrong, to be secure of the integrity of that information, and to have some sort of recourse if violations occur. Of course, firms that ignore consumer privacy run a tremendous risk when things go wrong. As Equifax and similar cases like Target prove, things *will* eventually go wrong (Dezenhall, 2015).

The privacy paradox

The privacy paradox stems from the observation that consumers express a strong desire to protect their privacy, but that some do not act like that desire is important. In practice, many consumers opt for convenience over privacy. For example, we allow Google to track our movements to make our use of Google Maps more efficient. We download apps that use the data on our phone, but tap the "Accept" button without reading the specific details. Privacy issues tend to get ignored until something goes wrong and then wrath may well be directed at the firm.

Many of the themes of digital marketing have a privacy component to them. For example, we all enjoy service specifically tailored to us. Digital processes allow for automation of this kind of personalization, but the question is, when does personalization move from being friendly to being creepy? Speaking of creepy, many students may have noticed that after shopping for a particular product, you start to see ads for that product appear on various other websites. We will discuss this technique, known as behavioral targeting, in Chapter 14. For now, we should ask ourselves whether it will create goodwill or fear and loathing on the part of our would-be customers.

One way that consumers have been fighting back against invasions of privacy is through encryption. Messaging apps such as WhatsApp employ encryption to prevent others from reading your messages. Unfortunately, encryption is the subject of much consternation on the part of governments everywhere. The reason for this? Governments are afraid that terrorists and other bad actors can use these apps to avoid detection.

Intellectual property

After privacy, issues pertaining to online intellectual property probably run a close second in terms of how often they appear in the business press. We now turn to such issues, starting with the idea of copyright.

Information products (discussed in Chapter 22) are easy to copy: a ubiquitous network creates the opportunity to copy and to distribute, and new file-sharing software can help people avoid arrest. It is no wonder that copyright is frequently in the news. US copyright laws protect the author or creator of a work for the author's lifetime plus 70 years, while the number varies in other countries. Note that one does not have to apply for copyright protection to any government agency. One need only assert copyright and that very act invokes the protection.

A second set of issues revolves around the notion of a trademark or service mark. Trademark law is quite different than copyright law. A trademark or service mark is a word, picture or symbol used to distinguish a company's offering. There are two ways to violate the trademark laws. One is through trademark dilution. This occurs when you do something to blur or weaken the connection between a company and its trademark. The second illegal act with respect to trademarks is known as tarnishment, which would seem to be self-explanatory. The concept of trade dress (Zugelder, 2005) means that it is possible to register the visual appearance of your entire website including color, design, symbols and graphics; in other words, look and feel.

Ambiguity about the exact relationship of a domain name with respect to a trademark is behind a host of Internet legal issues pertaining to cyber-squatting. In "real life," squatting occurs when someone takes over another's property, and cybersquatting is the virtual version of this crime. An example might occur were I to register a domain name for the purposes of extorting payments from the legitimate owner.

There are other ways in which the Internet's software runs up against trade-mark law. One way that search engines can categorize your page is with a meta tag (also covered in Chapter 22). One of the parameters of a meta tag is the keywords parameter, which allows site management to specify "key words" to help search engines categorize the site and decide if the page in question is relevant to the searcher. In general, the use of your trademark in other firms' meta tags is permitted if that use does not confuse the consumer. Likewise, there are issues surrounding search engine keyword purchases. Can I bid on Google for your firm's name to get people to see my search ad? Finally, the essence of the Web is the hyperlink, but the hyperlink itself can raise legal questions. Can I link to content on your website without acknowledging your site and bypassing your home page? Linking per se is not illegal unless it confuses the consumer. In most of the issues described in this section, consumer confusion seems to be the key element where the law draws a fairly bright line. If what you do has the potential to confuse consumers, the courts will not like it.

Location, location, location

For nearly 400 years it has seemed natural to think that the world is divided into mutually exclusive, geographically defined jurisdictions, and that any event can be unambiguously located on the surface of the Earth and there-fore within the jurisdiction of one state or another (Kobrin, 2001). This conceptualization was one of the results of the Thirty Years' War, which ended in 1648 with the Peace of Westphalia, and which marks the begin-ning of the modern territorial state. In the Western world, since 1648, the rules that apply to you depend on where you are. Software combined with networks lets us perform actions at a distance, simultaneously in more than one place, or perhaps nowhere specifically. For example, file-sharing software allows a file to be broken into pieces, encrypted and stored so that the pieces of the file are scattered across numerous computers attached to the file-sharing network in such a way that no participant knows what files are on their own machines. So, if the Recording Industry Association of America wants to know just where that illegally copied file is. . . it is everywhere and it is nowhere. A living human has to be in a specific well-defined geographic territory, but what occurs on a network does not, does it?

The location ambiguity of networks leads to a number of legal paradoxes. If I am in New Jersey and I bet on a horse race in Ireland using a company in France that has a server in Antigua while a bank in Kenya is holding my bet in escrow, where exactly did the transaction take place? This is not just a theoretical question. The future of hundreds of millions of tax dollars or euros could be at stake depending on the answer. Similarly, if the transaction goes wrong, where do I seek recourse? Whose laws apply in terms of recovery or remedy?

Taxes and recourse are not the only legal challenges associated with networks. In 2000, Yahoo! found itself defending its policies in front of the Tribunal de Grande Instance de Paris, a French criminal court (in *Ligue contre le racisme et l'antisémitisme et Union des étudiants juifs de France* v. *Yahoo! Inc. et Société Yahoo! France*). That court ruled that Yahoo! was guilty of breaking the French law that forbade vendors to offer Nazi memorabilia for sale. Indeed, the facts were clear that such merchandise had been offered for sale on Yahoo!'s auction site. Later, in *Yahoo.com, Inc.* v. *La Ligue contre le racisme et antisémitisme*, a California court ruled in favor of Yahoo!'s commercial First Amendment rights, but Yahoo! took down the offending material anyway. The interesting part of this case is the assertion by the French court system that it could regulate an American company that was doing business "in" France over the Internet. Another case (Re: MASTERCARD INTERNATIONAL INC., International Gambling Litigation decided in 2002) occurred when the US banned Internet gambling services based in other countries. Such jurisdictional cases are often referred to as involving the long arm of the law.

The importance of an ethics policy

So, we know that privacy is a key issue both from an ethical and legal point of view. We also know that digital networks create legal problems for companies. It is therefore important that marketers create an ethics policy for company digital activities before any such issues come up. Such policies need to have strong managerial support. The ethics policy should be as explicit as possible.

It might include a more general ethical code, but it should list detailed criteria as to what behaviors or actions are unethical. It is also important to spell out the consequences of unethical behavior. Another important requirement is that of a training program, and of creating constant motivation and the sense, among all employees, that ethics count as much as revenue.

Another way to prepare for the inevitable ethical dilemma is to have a set routine ready to go in case of an ethical issue. An ethical routine might start off with ascertaining the facts facing the firm. In some cases, what appears to be an ethical disagreement might just boil down to a simple question of facts. For this reason we should approach ethical dilemmas by trying to clarify what the facts actually are, and then it might be clearer why there is a dilemma or a disagreement.

Most ethical disagreements stem from a choice among several action alternatives facing the firm. It makes sense then to enumerate our action alternatives, and to sketch out what the likely consequences of each alternative might be. It is also useful to identify all stakeholders with respect to the disagreement and with respect to those consequences.

Any time you pick up a business newspaper or read a business story, the chances are that you will run into a question of ethics. In the past few years, companies such as Facebook and Google have been rocked by scandals involving fake news and hate speech. There are governments that censor the Internet. There are data that suggest that we are growing farther apart due to "filter bubbles." As a thinking human being, you are allowed to have your own opinion about all of these topics. But as a marketer, the one thing you are not allowed to do is ignore the ethical and legal implications of your firm's decisions. As a functional area, marketing is the discipline that represents the consumer to the firm, and represents the firm to the consumer. In effect, we are in the ideal position to insist on appropriate behavior of the companies we work for – behavior that encourages loyalty and a long-term relationship from our customers who trust us.

QUESTIONS AND EXERCISES

1 This question calls for dividing the class into teams, which will then engage in a series of short debates. A coin toss will determine who goes first. The first team gets two minutes, the second team gets two minutes, then each team gets a one-minute rebuttal. Your instructor can assign a position your team has to take, or the instructor might let you know which position you have to defend right before the debate. The issues are listed below. In a few cases these are current issues taken directly from the business section headlines, but in most cases these situations are completely hypothetical. Here are the issues:

(a) Internet gambling – should the US accede to the World Trade Organization's require-ment that it treats foreign gambling sites the same as US sites. The pro side should argue yes it should.

(b) Google vs American Airlines – should Google be able to sell "american airlines" as a keyword to Delta Airlines or Expedia? The pro side should argue that Google should be allowed to make these sales.

(c) Should e-tailers pay taxes just like offline retailers? The pro side should argue that e-tail-ers should indeed pay taxes like everyone else.

(d) Should the site www.foxnews.com accept censorship imposed by the Chinese govern-ment or risk losing a huge market opportunity? The pro side should argue yes.

(e) Should Fuji be allowed to include the word "Kodak" in a meta tag? The pro side should argue yes.

(f) Should Kodak be allowed to register the domain name fuji-is-second-rate.com? The pro side should argue that it ought to be allowed.

(g) Should Nissan Computer Company be required to post a notice that it was not affiliated with Nissan Motor Company? The pro side should argue that it must post the notice.

(h) Should it be illegal to post the software program that allows users to break the copy protection on the next generation of DVDs? The pro side should argue that it should be illegal to post such a key.

(i) When visitors provide their email address on your site, should they be asked to opt-in or opt-out of future email promotions from your firm? The pro side should argue for opt-in while the con side should argue for opt-out.

(j) China has attempted to censor Google search results. Should Google pull out of the China market? The pro side should say yes while the con side should say no.

2 Kraut et al. (1998) have noted that television tends to reduce social involvement and civic par-ticipation while the telephone tends to enhance social participation. Where does the Internet fit in? Does it reduce or enhance social involvement and participation? Of course you should justify your answer.

3 Assume that you work as a digital marketer for a company that sells consumer electronics online. Write up a potential online ethics policy for this company. Recall that an ethics policy should include detailed criteria as to what is unethical along with predetermined consequences for unethical behavior.

4 Try to locate the ethics or privacy policy for two different companies that you are familiar with. If you find such a policy, summarize it. If you cannot find one, pick a site and write a policy for that site.

5 In some publicized cases what appeared to be consumer-generated content was actually paid content with companies footing the bill. So, for example, a movie production company might pay someone to pose as a normal theatergoer and write a glowing review of that company's new film. Or a gadget maker might pay a large group of "consumers" to tweet about the gadget maker's newest product. In your opinion, how ethical are these behaviors? How might we use the concepts of this chapter to judge them or to decide whether firms should use such tactics?

 REFERENCES

Dezenhall, E. (2015), "A look back at the Target breach," *Huffington Post*, March 6, accessed February 6, 2018 at https://www.huffingtonpost.com/eric-dezenhall/a-look-back-at-the-target _b_7000816.html.

Kobrin, S.J. (2001), "Territoriality and the governance of cyberspace," *Journal of International Business Studies*, **32** (4), 687–704.

Kraut, R., M. Patterson and V. Lundmark et al. (1998), "Internet paradox: A social technology that reduces social involvement and psychological well-being?" *American Psychologist*, **53** (9), 1017–31.

Lieber, R. (2017), "How to protect yourself after the Equifax breach," *New York Times*, October 16, accessed February 6, 2018 at https://www.nytimes.com/interactive/2017/your-money/equifax-data-breach-credit.html.

Wolf, J. (2017), "Roomba vacuum maker iRobot betting big on the 'smart' home," *Reuters*, July 24, accessed September 6, 2017 at https://www.reuters.com/article/us-irobot-strategy/roomba-vacuum-maker-irobot-betting-big-on-the-smart-home-idUSKBN1A91A5.

Zugelder, M.T. (2005), "Legal online marketing issues: Opportunities and challenges," in I. Clarke III and T.B. Flaherty (eds), *Advances in Electronic Marketing*, Hershey, PA: The Idea Group.

6

Internal company operations

We start this chapter with a brief look at how businesses have adopted information technology (IT) over the past decades. Of course, the backdrop of this adoption is the historic price deflation in IT gear that became especially noticeable with the invention of the transistor in 1947. But deflation in IT prices means that any and all firms can buy the latest stuff inexpensively. So how do firms achieve any sort of sustainable competitive advantage from IT? Answering that question takes up the second part of this chapter. The chapter finishes up with a discussion of how firms are using intranet technology to pursue organizational goals.

Historical background

Investment in IT became a mainstream business strategy in the early to mid-1960s, but business organizations began to see real information technology-driven change beginning in the early 1980s. The Apple II personal computer series was introduced in 1977 followed by the IBM PC in 1981. This second machine legitimized the PC for business since IBM was the dominant provider of IT to the corporate world. Putting computers on everybody's desktop did not, at first, help companies reduce costs, but when these desktop machines were connected into local area networks (LANs), corporations started to realize reductions in coordination costs (discussed in detail in Chapter 8). The LAN boom was sparked by the Ethernet standard (see Chapter 3), which offered a commodity-like and inexpensive method for creating short-haul networks within buildings, beginning in the mid-1980s. During this time, firms flattened (Evans and Wurster, 1997), which is to say, they eliminated middle management positions as the necessity for "pushing paper" became obsolete. Next, these LANs were combined into Internet Protocol-based networks beginning in the early 1990s. We next saw the promulgation of off-the-shelf intranet applications starting in the mid-1990s. At that point, the connectivity that had been developed for intra-firm communication began to extend outwards toward suppliers and business-to-business (B2B) clients and then eventually toward customers like you and me.

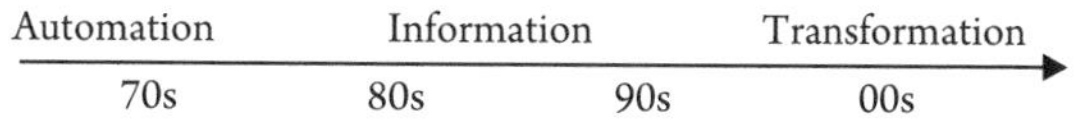

Figure 6.1 The time sequence of IT-based business transformation. After Brady (2003)

Automation	Information	Transformation
70s	80s 90s	00s

There was a long lag between the time that firms began to heavily invest in IT and the time they figured out how to deploy it to reduce costs. For individual firms to realize productivity gains, one could argue that the entire economy had to develop sufficient knowledge and experience with information systems. What's more, a new technology infrastructure was needed, with new categories of resellers, clusters of expertise, service firms, repair capabilities, programmers, systems analysts, wiring and even new types of furniture. Most of all, what was needed were new ways of doing things by companies – new ways of organizing work. In many cases, externalities existed with the new technology. In other words, the benefits received by one firm in adopting the new technology depended on how many other firms adopted it. Naturally, all these factors slowed the process. All the while, firms had to learn by doing – receiving any benefits required sufficient first-hand experience.

So, one can say that it took quite a while before firms figured out how to use IT to automate previously existing processes and thus save money. But this was itself just a baby step! Then firms figured out how to use technology to provide more information to management. Only in the late 1990s did businesses begin to truly transform themselves on the basis of IT (Brady, 2003). This time sequence is illustrated in Figure 6.1.

Sustainable competitive advantage

Of course, firms want to use technology as a tool to generate sustainable competitive advantage. According to the resource-based view of the firm (see Hunt and Morgan, 1995 for a marketing application of this view), firms need resources that are valuable, rare, inimitable and non-substitutable (VRIN). Unfortunately, IT, by its nature, quickly becomes a commodity that anyone can buy. Thus, it is difficult to create a sustainable advantage based on the technology you buy. However, we must make a distinction between two different types of resources: assets and capabilities. Assets consist of both tangible assets (like IT infrastructure) and intangible assets (like reputation, image, brand equity). Next, there is a completely different type of resource, known as a capability. A capability is the ability to combine assets in a strategically logical way (Wade and Hulland, 2004). In effect, a capability is a competence to array one's assets in the competitive arena. Capabilities also include processes and routines that firms have learned to perform. While assets, especially tangible assets like computers and networks, can simply be bought, the capability to put them together to create a strategy requires learning by doing. Such slowly acquired know-how is valuable, rare, inimitable and non-substitutable (VRIN)!

So, the upshot is that investment in IT is necessary for firms to stay even with the competition, but by itself does not guarantee success. Any purchased technology must be modified to work together with other assets to solve specific strategic problems. When IT and business strategies match, we can say that the firm is aligned (Henderson and Venkatraman, 1993).

Intranets

Today most companies use Internet technology internally. IP and related protocols, when employed inside a firm and protected by password access, are collectively known as an intranet, which is defined as follows:

> An intranet is an IP network used for internal company purposes, and which is usually closed to outsiders.

Intranets can be used to organize digital assets to create and enhance employee collaboration, coordination and productivity. Many, but not all, the software applications in use in intranets closely resemble the open Internet we all use as part of our daily lives. Companies use:

- enterprise resource planning;
- the Web browser as a kiosk for enterprise-wide data;
- knowledge management;
- content management and document sharing;
- sales-led development systems;
- trouble ticket service failure databases;
- calendaring applications;
- audio-video teleconferencing;
- whiteboard and netmeeting software;
- email, chat, texting and messaging;
- web-board and email listservs;
- workflow management; and
- customer relationship management systems (see Chapter 7).

Firms often use their IP networks to implement the client–server model discussed in Chapter 3. The server holds key company data and the client is used to facilitate decision making. This allows employees to be more efficient when they engage in search and in general helps with the management of knowledge. Intranets also give access to shared experience and data, create a medium for in-house online training, help with project management, and prepare and filter raw Internet data.

One important intranet contribution is that it can be used to enhance employee collaboration and team coordination. With access to the right data, employees can be empowered to better serve the customer. Kiosks now appear in many stores, allowing sales associates to access company data. Well-run firms create a cadre of trained employees with decentralized authority to solve customer problems using IT. Where these employees are located matters less each year. Firms employ virtual teams consisting of groups of workers from any time zone working together using email, calendaring, and the rest of the above list.

Marketers can use an intranet to communicate product information, specifications, to archive key market research results, for customer prospecting, for managing sales contacts and for sales training. In addition to marketing, HR, Accounting, Finance, Manufacturing and Operations can all share information this way, breaking down functional silos and creating synergy across the firm.

The existence of these functional silos should not be allowed to block key digital assets. One critical type of digital asset is the firm's customer data. Customer data should be allowed, assuming appropriate security and privacy guarantees, to flow across the firm's different retail and communication channels. Customer databases will be discussed further in Chapter 7, but for now let's just say that there should be a single view of the customer regardless of the channel and regardless of how or why the data were originally collected. Other key digital assets include artwork, photographs, product descriptions and advertisement copy. Ideally, these could be reused in a variety of different applications.

Well-run firms function at a faster clock speed than do run-of-the-mill firms. They change and innovate more quickly, allowing them to better react to opportunities. Faster clock speed can be achieved with intranets that are designed to help in environmental, customer and competitive scanning, to help sense opportunities, to bring these opportunities to management's attention no matter who is the source of the insight, and to quickly design and implement an effective offering. An intranet is the firm's nervous system. Faster internal connectivity makes for a nimbler, more alert firm.

To sum up, intranets are a tangible asset that can be employed to keep marketers aware of the current marketing environment and to alert them to threats or opportunities. The basic hardware and software for intranets are becoming less expensive. It is also true that the technology necessary to use the Internet for communicating, for selling, or for enabling connections, has become less expensive. Firms find it much harder to create the capabilities to array this technology in the quest to satisfy customers better. This requires know-how. Like the know-how that you are acquiring in this class!

 QUESTIONS AND EXERCISES

1 Give a hypothetical example of where a company uses the Internet to automate a process to reduce costs.
2 Give a hypothetical example of where a company uses the Internet to provide better information to management so that those managers can make better decisions in a timely fashion.
3 Give a concrete example of where a company uses the Internet to transform itself or an entire industry, creating a competitive advantage.
4 Why do you suppose business people are heavy users of email while students are heavy users of text messaging and chat?

REFERENCES

Brady, M. (2003), "Managing information technology," *Irish Journal of Management*, **24** (1), 125–38.

Evans, P.B. and T.S. Wurster (1997), "Strategy and the new economics of information," *Harvard Business Review*, **75** (5), 70–82.

Henderson, J.C. and N. Venkatraman (1993), "Strategic alignment: Leveraging information technology for transforming organizations," *IBM Systems Journal*, **32** (1), 4–16.

Hunt, S.D. and R.M. Morgan (1995), "The comparative advantage theory of competition," *Journal of Marketing*, **59** (2), 1–15.

Wade, M. and J. Hulland (2004), "The resource-based view and information systems research: Review, extension, and suggestions for future research," *MIS Quarterly*, **28** (1), 107–14.

Digital networks as a communications medium

Electronic networks can be used for advertising and communication analogous to traditional mass media. But, unlike traditional media, interactive media allow for complex communication patterns, where firms can talk to consumers, consumers can talk to firms, and consumers can talk to each other. Such complexity is well suited to building relationships, and relationships form an important theme of this section. The relationship theme becomes even more important when we contemplate the ways that websites and mobile apps can help the consumer. In this sense, interactive media are not just for communication; they can provide supplemental services of many sorts.

After covering B2C and then B2B relationships in Chapters 7 and 8, we move on to discussing the design of firm–customer interaction. In designing such interaction, the focus is on the customer – the customer's resources, capabilities and motivations (Chapters 9 and 10). Then follow three chapters on owned media, comprising a chapter on visual aspects of screen design (Chapter 11), one on verbal aspects of screen design (Chapter 12), and how pages or screens within a site or app connect to each other (Chapter 13). A second theme of this section is the three levels of interaction design: the overall site, the page, and the individual links and words that are found on pages. The section ends with a chapter on interactive advertising (Chapter 14), thereby capping off the three chapters on owned media with a chapter on paid media.

7

Consumer–business relationships

For years, we marketers have used the mass media to talk at our customers, to blast out messages that for the most part those customers did their best to avoid. We find ourselves in a different situation with interactive digital media. For one thing, the client–server architecture (discussed in Chapter 3) allows us to go beyond talking; we can do something useful for the customer in the form of complementary services (see Chapter 2). For another thing, the customer, rather than sitting in front of a television set, finds themselves in front of a powerful computational device with upwards of a billion transistors. The Web, as we see from Chapter 3, is user driven, meaning that the user employs this computational power to do pretty much whatever he or she wants, choosing what to look at. This is becoming truer of mobile devices as well. If the message isn't right, there is always the old back arrow. What's more, the Internet not only allows us to communicate with the user, it allows the user to communicate with us.

Rather than pretend that nothing has changed between the 1950s and today, we need to accept that the playing field between us and our customers has leveled. We can no longer talk *at* them. We need to establish a true relationship and create a conversation on that basis. The theme of this chapter is therefore relationships. We start by exploring the nature of relationships and go from there to talking about how to manage them. After that, we talk about managing the digital data that are naturally created from relationships and how we can use those data to understand the value of each of our relationships and act accordingly.

Marketing relationships

The classic economic theory of transactional exchange in mass markets assumes that all customers are identical, and that each transaction between a firm and a customer is executed in isolation, without taking into account the relationship between them. The technology that enables online

Figure 7.1 A simplified model of repatronage

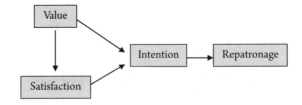

communication allows for addressability. Unlike mass media, digital networks let us address customers individually, understand customers individually, and put the relationship between our firm and these customers at the top of the marketing agenda. Technology has therefore helped marketing move away from the classic economic theory of transactional exchange and towards a new theory of relational exchange.

The way in which relationships have become a strategic imperative is illustrated by Harrah's Las Vegas. Harrah's created a database of 24 million gamblers that was used to generate website and email marketing. Access to the website is connected, via a login id, with information on how much a player spends on Harrah's properties. Each player is offered tailored hotel and recreation deals. Such a tactic fills Harrah's hotels and optimizes Harrah's gambling earnings.

We define a relationship as a long-lasting, mutually beneficial connection between the firm and the customer. Marketers try to integrate all activities toward establishing, developing and maintaining successful relational exchanges. By definition, a strong, loyal relationship implies customer retention or repatronage, which leads to increased profitability. Here Figure 7.1 shows part of Figure 2.1 from Chapter 2. You can see that value and satisfaction drive customers to reward the firm with loyal behavior.

Sawhney and Zabin (2002) highlight four stages to the relationship life cycle:

1. **Attract:** Identify and invest, create joint goals.
2. **Retain:** Deepen loyalty, educate, encourage relationship-specific investments. Retention or repatronage is a key theme of Chapter 2.
3. **Extend:** Broaden the relationship, new or complementary products and channels.
4. **Leverage:** Referrals, resell third-party offerings, increase prices.

A good relationship acts to create switching costs for the consumer (Burnham, Frels and Mahajan, 2003). Online, the act of learning how to navigate a website can make other sites less attractive and thereby work in favor of customer retention. In other words, a customer's time investment in learning your site or app can create an obstacle blocking other sites from luring that customer away. Maintaining relationships has become quite important in marketing, so that is the subject of the next section.

Customer relationship management

The emphasis on relationships, combined with an increasing use of company IT infrastructure (see Chapter 6) has led to an important reorientation in marketing away from product management and towards customer relationship management (CRM). Customer relationship management has therefore begun to replace the four Ps (product, price, promotion and place) as a central organizing philosophy of marketing. According to Swift (2001):

> CRM is a strategic posture calling for iterative processes designed to turn customer data into customer relationships through active use of, and learning from, the information collected.

The move towards CRM puts emphasis on performing marketing using customer information databases (called, cleverly enough, database marketing). There is also emphasis on using databases to measure the value of, and for, each customer. The customer tries to assess the value of the firm's offerings but the firm also assesses the value of the customer. This is known as the dual value process.

Next, we cover the database aspects of CRM and their importance to marketing. After that, we talk about the dual value process and how marketers can measure the financial value of a relationship with a customer.

Digital data

The philosophy of relationship marketing tells us that information about customers may ultimately be more valuable to us than any particular transaction. For example, Amazon uses information about previous purchases to cross-sell books of possible interest to other customers. Data are fundamental to relationship marketing and in fact allow us to attract, retain, extend and leverage relationships.

Data are often stored in a data warehouse. A data warehouse allows for storage and retrieval of all two-way communications between the firm and the customer, along with all the data generated by sales. Psychological or

Figure 7.2 A
hypothetical example of
a relational database

Customer Records

cust_id	address	age
32882	33 J St	23
75676	1 H St	32
88842	4 L St	55

Product Records

prod_id	desc
4A887	hammer
7V266	nail

Transaction Records

cust_id	date	prod_id
75676	1–7–14	7V266
32882	1–8–14	4A887

demographic information may also be available from surveys, list brokers, or public data sources.

Such data may be saved in the form of a flat file, which contains a single rectangular table, or in a relational database. A typical rectangular table, like a customer table, might have a separate row for each customer and a separate column for each customer characteristic (e.g., age). A relational database (illustrated in Figure 7.2), on the other hand, consists of multiple tables, and the accompanying software that can be used to access data in more than one table, and to relate data elements from those tables. In general, each table will have a key field. For example, a set of transaction records may have one row for each purchase, and a column for the product id, and another column for the customer id. Thus, each data record or row provides all the detail needed to recreate a specific purchase. That same customer id will appear in a customer table including demographic information, allowing us to link customer demographics to purchase records and produce reports about the characteristics of people who have purchased certain products.

Demographics, of course, are not the be all and end all of marketing data. It would be especially useful to know the following about customers:

- customer preferences – which brands or services the customer likes;
- customer attribute importance weights – what product attributes matter to the customer;

- consideration sets – which offerings the customer might contemplate buying; and
- cognitive style – how the customer goes about making purchase decisions.

All the above items are discussed in Chapter 15, which looks at consumer problem solving. These might be inferred and stored based on customers' website interactions and from their purchases on the site. In addition to those psychological variables, some additional essentials should be in the data warehouse, including:

- transaction information;
- contact history;
- marketing exposure history; and
- product usage.

For example, data from a customer might include records of calls to the call center, website visits, kiosk use, app use, automated voice response system calls, contact with sales associates and customer service reps, cash register records, email and SMS messages sent and received, and various point-of-service card swipes.

Once data have been collected, we might use them for five different purposes: enterprise reporting, personalization, customization, data mining and analytical modeling:

- **Customization:** The firm can allow the customer to create the product, or any 4P elements.
- **Personalization:** If I have a record of your preferences, importance weights, and the other items described above, I can dynamically modify my site to provide you with a personalized experience. The notion here is that each customer sees a slightly different version of the page, the site, or the interface, a version optimized to their personal requirements. I can figure out how to customize your experience using the next three processes, but especially data mining and analytical modeling.
- **Enterprise reporting:** Software designed for this task compiles the data from all customer touch points. Reports produced by this software can provide a snapshot of customer and marketing activity and allow managers to monitor marketing programs and their effectiveness.
- **Data mining:** Data mining refers to an automated post hoc (not based on hypotheses) search for patterns in the above information. Software can look for relationships among the various fields or variables stored

in different tables in the data warehouse, and since this process is highly automated, the technique is part of an approach sometimes called machine learning. For example, Wal-Mart has used its 460 terabyte data warehouse to discover that the number one product sold just before a hurricane is beer, and that the pre-hurricane sales of Strawberry Pop-Tarts go up by a factor of seven (Hays, 2004). Data mining (machine learning) can also be used to discover the existence of segments. Data mining is often used when there is a large amount of customer data. In that case, the analyst can divide the copious amount of data into two sets: a training set and a testing set. The training set is used to come up with interesting approaches to understanding the data and the testing set is used to test whether the approaches are valid or not. Blattberg, Kim and Neslin (2008) cover many of the techniques for mining customer data.

- **Analytical modeling:** Data mining searches for post hoc relationships. In other words, it is used to look for associations after the fact. Analytical modeling is used to better understand marketing data by hypothesizing cause-and-effect relationships a priori. In other words, before the fact. Models typically incorporate an objective function and at least one decision variable. A decision variable is something that can vary that we marketers have control over. What should my price be? How many operators should I have standing by? Which page format should I use? An objective function is a variable that serves as a measure of success. Digital marketing examples of objective functions might include the number of repeat site visits by customers, number of photo uploads, frequency of profile updates or other contributions, messages sent, online transaction volume or unit sales, time on site, page views, or banners clicked.

One very important objective function summarizes the profitability of the firm–customer relationship and is known as customer equity. We now turn to this variable.

Customer equity

While marketers have always tried to understand value from the consumer's point of view, valuing the customer is a new way (new from the late 1990s; Berger and Nasr, 1998) for us to think about marketing. Customer equity is the amount of profit that we can expect from all our customers in the future and thus serves to quantify the value of our market. This allows us to prioritize our marketing efforts. Where should we put our money to maximize customer equity? Will additional spending on advertising increase equity more than the same amount spent on quality improvement?

The notion of customer equity is especially important when thinking about targeting and segmentation. Why would Harrah's spend a large amount of its money on a customer who only gambles a few coins at a time? It wants to reward large clients, not small players. Here we present two basic ways of assessing the value of individual customers:

Scoring model

A scoring model produces a next-period prediction of response, often based on three variables: recency, frequency and monetary value (RFM). A customer is scored as being more valuable if he or she has recently purchased, if he or she has frequently purchased, and if he or she has spent a large monetary value.

Customer lifetime value

Customer lifetime value (CLV) is the net present value of the predicted future revenue stream for a specific customer. Thus, CLV allows us to conceptualize and measure the equity or value stored in one individual. CLV can then be summed over all customers to estimate customer equity. Below is a simple equation for CLV inspired by Jain and Singh (2002) and Kumar, Ramani and Bohling (2004):

$$\text{CLV} = \sum_{t=0}^{\infty} \frac{G_t - C_t}{(1+i)^t} R^t$$

In the numerator of the equation for customer lifetime value, we see the net customer contribution for period t, consisting of the gross sales (G) minus the costs (C) for each period t. The i in the denominator represents the interest or discount rate, while R is the expected customer retention rate. A value near 1.0 for R implies that we have no customer churn (rate of attrition), while a value closer to zero means that we lose almost all our customers every year. This financial equation allows us to quantify the predicted contribution of each customer to the firm's bottom line. We might note here that while the RFM scoring model and the notion of CLV are discussed in this chapter on consumer relationships, they are also, and perhaps more so, used in a B2B context (see Chapter 8).

Any spending by the firm that increases customer equity may be thought of as an investment and justified by the return on that investment. In contrast, an accountant may think that increasing service levels is merely a "cost." If a marketer can use analytical modeling to show there is a positive return on this investment, the marketer can better represent the customer inside the boardroom and insure the long-term viability of the firm. Customization is an example of where we invest in differentiation to grow equity. Another example, albeit a less dynamic one, is the loyalty program.

Loyalty programs

Maintaining a high level of customer lifetime value is one goal of frequent buyer programs. These can help us (Università Bocconi, 2005):

- raise switching costs, which enhances retention;
- avoid price competition and dealing;
- create barriers to entry for new firms;
- generate trust as the firm learns more;
- capture panel-like data to better understand consumer behavior;
- capture data to understand market structure;
- use data for customization; and
- create cross-selling opportunities.

What are the problems with these programs? Unfortunately, loyalty programs:

- don't work for change-of-pace brands;
- don't work for low-involvement products;
- can lock-in the customer, but also locks the firm into the loyalty program;
- create loyalty to the program, not the brand; and
- can be easily imitated.

? QUESTIONS AND EXERCISES

1 This chapter discusses Harrah's Las Vegas who offered tailored hotel and recreation deals to their clients. How might the company choose the hotel price for a particular client? If you were to sort all Harrah's customers with the best customer first, and the worst customer last, how would you do that?

2 The economic concept of elasticity has traditionally guided marketers trying to decide how much to invest in sales promotion, advertising, along with other decision variables. We might consider as an example a firm trying to decide whether to email electronic coupons to be used by customers in their next online purchase. A redeemed coupon costs the firm the face value of that coupon, but it might be considered an investment. Elasticity provides us with one guideline as to whether this investment is worth it. The impact on CLV provides a competing guideline as to whether the investment is worth it. What is the difference between the economic concept of elasticity and the marketing concept of customer lifetime value? Which formula provides the most logical basis for making marketing decisions and why?

3 In the equation for customer lifetime value, why does customer equity appear to go down over time? In other words, why do future sales appear to be worth less than current sales? How does

the interest rate assumed change the equity? What value should we plug in for the interest rate in this equation?

4   If you were going to create a more complex analytical model based on the customer equity equation, what decision variables might you add to the model that would influence R, the retention rate? What decision variables could we include that might influence G, the gross contribution?

(a)   Do this assuming a website whose purpose is selling or e-tail.

(b)   Do this assuming a website whose purpose is communicating, or advertising a product sold only offline.

(c)   Do this assuming a website whose purpose is to connect article writers with advertisers, like the *Wall Street Journal* site.

5   Think about the last online purchase you made, and the site you used. What data might have been generated by that transaction?

6   How might we change the concept of customer lifetime value if we wanted to take into account word-of-mouth processes? So, consider a customer who is always saying very positive things about your company on Facebook. How might we take that into account when assessing the value of that customer?

7   This chapter describes the relationship life cycle of Sawhney and Zabin (2002), consisting of the following four stages: attract, retain, extend and leverage. How might a grocery store, one that sells only offline, use a website for each of these four stages?

 REFERENCES

Berger, P.D. and N.I. Nasr (1998), "Customer lifetime value: Marketing models and applications," *Journal of Interactive Marketing*, **12** (1), 17–30.

Blattberg, R.C., B.-D. Kim and S.A. Neslin (2008), *Database Marketing: Analyzing and Managing Customers* (International Series in Quantitative Marketing), New York: Springer.

Burnham, T.A., J.K. Frels and V. Mahajan (2003), "Consumer switching costs: A typology, antecedents, and consequences," *Journal of the Academy of Marketing Science*, **31** (2), 109–26.

Hays, C.L. (2004), "What Wal-Mart knows about customers' habits," *New York Times*, November 14, accessed November 28, 2008 at http://www.nytimes.com/2004/11/14/business/yourmoney/14wal.html.

Jain, D.C. and S.S. Singh (2002), "Customer lifetime value research in marketing: A review and future directions," *Journal of Interactive Marketing*, **16** (2), 34–46.

Kumar, V., G. Ramani and T. Bohling (2004), "Customer lifetime value: Approaches and best practice applications," *Journal of Interactive Marketing*, **18** (3), 60–72.

Sawhney, M. and J. Zabin (2002), "Managing and measuring relational equity in the network economy," *Journal of the Academy of Marketing Science*, **30** (4), 313–32.

Swift, R.S. (2001), *Accelerating Customer Relationships Using CRM and Relationship Technologies*, Upper Saddle River, NJ: Prentice Hall.

Università Bocconi (2005), Unpublished Teaching Note, Marketing Area, Scuola di Direzione Aziendale.

8

Business–business relationships

Businesses increasingly depend on other businesses for key inputs. We will see much evidence for this later, in Chapter 21, when we look at supply chains. This fundamental fact means that the opportunities for B2B marketing are on the increase. The reasons for this increasing reliance on other firms will be the topic of the last section in this chapter. For now, we note that supplier and buyer firms in today's economy tend to rely on each other as never before, and therefore require a strong commitment from each other. The supplying firm needs to telegraph this commitment as part of its marketing program and the buying firm needs to know that the seller is indeed committed. Technology enters into this equation since commitment depends on trust, and trust in turn depends on communication, as suggested by Morgan and Hunt (1994) and shown in Figure 8.1.

Figure 8.1 The commitment-trust theory of relationship marketing. After Morgan and Hunt (1994)

As the Internet and technology in general drive down the cost of communicating, we might surmise from Morgan and Hunt's theory that businesses will be able to trust each other more than in the past. This will lead to higher levels of commitment in business-to-business relationships. Less costly communication can also allow B2B marketers to better see the world the way their customers do and help to anticipate their customers' needs.

B2B relationships compared with B2C relationships

Commitment is not the only aspect of B2B marketing that differs from B2C marketing. In fact, business marketing has many unique features not shared with consumer marketing (see Bridges, Goldsmith and Hofacker,

2005 for an overview). B2B exchange typically involves more complex negotiations that might even include some sort of reciprocity or barter. In many cases, buyer–seller business relationships resemble collaboration more than selling, so a B2B marketer plays a role as a partner to the client as much as the role of salesperson. B2B exchange generally involves fewer customers, with larger sales volumes for each customer. This implies that individual B2B relationships are more valuable than individual B2C relationships, and firms therefore make a greater investment in those relationships, relying more on direct channels, on personal selling, and less on impersonal advertising. The sales function in many B2B firms puts a human face on the firm's valuable market contacts. These days, LinkedIn can be used to facilitate contact, as is described in Chapter 25. Human investment in specific clients is further justified when we consider that B2B buyers tend to have very high customer lifetime value (Chapter 7), high information needs, and are often seeking specific benefits. Ironically, personal contact is so important in B2B that marketers often employ a variety of automated tools to allocate the time of the sales force and to help the buying firm. Such sales force automation software can be used to schedule and track client contact opportunities, deal with inventory, see which employees are hitting their targets, reduce the time involved in the sales cycle, and generate new leads.

Even in a single one-shot B2B sale, there may be multiple buyers and influences involved. In the case of larger firms, the buyers are professional – it is their job to buy things for their firm. But a variety of individuals playing different roles might participate in a firm's purchasing decision. These roles might include the initiator, decider, influencer, purchaser, gatekeeper and user (Bonoma, 1982).

We can divide B2B purchasing into two main categories: direct and indirect inputs. Direct inputs represent the larger of the two categories in monetary terms, and consist of components, parts, labor and raw materials that directly go into the production process. Indirect inputs include maintenance, repair and "operations" items. We might use as an example of a direct input the steel that Ford buys for its autos, but Ford also needs indirect inputs like pencils, mops and computers. Of course, both types of inputs can be services. When we consider B2B services such as spare parts management, order processing and fulfillment, financial processing, warehouse management, cleaning, refrigeration, inventory control, repair, return, transport, cloud IT services, payroll and so on, we can see why services are an important part of the B2B world, just as they are in the business-to-consumer (B2C) space.

Extranets

The process of purchasing involves a series of steps: search, qualify, negotiate, purchase order, invoice, ship and remit payment. Many of these steps can be made faster and executed more effectively through the use of an extranet, defined as follows:

> The extranet is the use of an IP network to enhance the collaborative relationship between allied firms and buyers and sellers, and which is usually closed to non-participants.

Internet technology applied to a B2B relationship can speed the procurement process, giving both firms literally second-by-second updates on price changes, as well as on sales forecasts, product specifications, and shipping information. In addition, this allows the firms involved to perform data mining and analytical modeling, to accelerate organizational learning, and makes the supply chain more transparent and therefore more responsive to business customer needs.

Often direct inputs are purchased by long-term sourcing while indirect inputs are more likely to be acquired via spot markets and multiple suppliers using auctions (see Chapter 20). Thus, extranets are especially relevant for direct inputs. If we are a firm selling direct inputs to other businesses, the goal of our extranet is not just to sell to these customers, but to collaborate with them, to partner with them, making them more profitable. The extranet is a channel by which we can provide supplementary services to our business customers.

Not only are we competing against other firms to produce superior service, but in some cases we are also competing with our customer, who might decide to create or produce the product or service in question itself. This leads us to think about the make-or-buy decision. What drives firms to get a good or a service from outside the firm? When and why do firms outsource instead of producing a service or good themselves? This is the next topic.

Outsourcing

Why are companies the size they are instead of much bigger or much smaller? Another way to ask the question is as follows: how do firms decide whether to make or produce something for themselves, or whether to purchase that item or service from another firm? Obviously, if firms made or produced everything they ever needed, they would need to be much bigger. Conversely, theoretically, firms might consist solely of a president who outsources everything, except being presidential of course. Diving into this most fundamental question requires that we separate two kinds of costs faced by businesses: (1) production cost – the cost of the primary processes necessary to create goods or services; and (2) coordination cost – the cost of governance or administration, or the cost of coordinating people or machines so they can create goods or services.

A firm chooses between make or buy based on the total of the two costs. A hierarchy (control by managerial authority, i.e., "make") leads to low coordination costs but high production costs. Markets (controlled by price, i.e., "buy") lead to high coordination costs but low production costs.

Why are production costs higher within firms than in markets? Third-party firms might enjoy economies of scale, and might in fact specialize in the particular good or service being outsourced. These firms must compete with other such firms, and competition frequently keeps prices lower.

Why are coordination costs higher in markets than within firms? The buying firm must search for sellers, negotiate, monitor the contract and monitor the financial settlement. The seller must advertise and search for buyers.

But digital networks reduce coordination costs! Extranets are not expensive so the cost of information exchange and coordination is low. We can implement automatic procurement, automatic reordering, delivery tracking, monitoring, and inventory control and balance.

All these technological aids reduce the main impediments to outsourcing, and ever cheaper digital communication leads to increased communication, which then leads to higher trust. The end result is a series of opportunities for B2B marketers. Here is an example from transportation services. Businesses can either have a large shipping department, or outsource this function to companies such as FedEx. Federal Express helps its B2B clients in many ways, including educating them, providing technology for them and acting as a good partner, trying to help those clients become more profitable. FedEx uses the Internet to increase the trust in the job it is doing by letting clients see – in real time – exactly where their packages are. This lets those clients be more responsive to their own customers and keeps everybody happy.

You have probably heard the expression, "It's not what you know, it's who you know." While this may not be true in some fields, in B2B marketing there is some truth to it. Business relationships are another form of network, where the nodes are individuals and the arcs represent business relationships.

Figure 8.2 An example of a structural hole (between B and C). A can take advantage of a brokerage opportunity

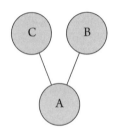

Suppose person A is connected to B and A is also connected to C but B is not connected to C. The lack of a network arc (Figure 8.2) between B and C provides A with additional power in the form of a brokerage opportunity. The lack of this arc is often referred to as a structural hole. In a world in which networks are becoming ubiquitous, the wise marketer nurtures business relationships offline and online.

Speaking of who you know, B2B marketers tend to use different social networks than B2C marketers. As was mentioned above, there is less emphasis on Facebook and more emphasis on LinkedIn and similar platforms that are more professionally focused. Similarly, blogging is a great digital marketing tool for any product categories that tend to be technical and detail oriented; precisely those kinds of product categories that one business sells to another.

 QUESTIONS AND EXERCISES

1   The process of purchasing can be broken down into the following steps: search, qualify, negotiate, purchase order, invoice, ship and remit payment. How might an extranet help with each one of these tasks?
2   An asset that a company needs might be unusual or specific to that firm, or it might be a very common commodity. An asset that is unique is said to be a specific asset. How does the specificity of the asset relate to the likelihood that a firm will make or produce it (versus buy or outsource it)?
3   Dividing up business purchases into direct and indirect inputs, how do you suppose that business relationships will vary from one to the other?
4   One factor that reduces outsourcing is the fear of opportunism, defined as behaviors by the selling firm to maximize short-term profits at the expense of the buying firm. Where might we see opportunism? Do digital networks mitigate against opportunism, or increase the opportunities for it?

REFERENCES

Bonoma, T.V. (1982), "Major sales: Who really does the buying?" *Harvard Business Review*, **60** (3), 111–19.

Bridges, E., R.E. Goldsmith and C.F. Hofacker (2005), "Attracting and retaining online buyers: Comparing B2C and B2B customers," in I. Clarke III and T.B. Flaherty (eds), *Advances in Electronic Marketing*, Hershey, PA: The Idea Group.

Morgan, R.M. and S.D. Hunt (1994), "The commitment-trust theory of relationship marketing," *Journal of Marketing*, **58** (3), 20–38.

9

The online audience

Designing websites has always been difficult. We know this because only 61.2 percent of websites present in 1997 were still around five years later (McMillan, 2002). More recently, Kenkai (2007) checked to see how many sites that had asked for a free search engine positioning report in 2004 were still around three years later. The answer was only 41 percent. I imagine that you personally hear people complaining about websites and mobile apps fairly often. Jupiter Media Metrix asked consumers in 2001 to provide their main complaints about the websites they visit. The values on the right in Table 9.1 represent the percentage of the sample mentioning each problem:

Note that among the list of common complaints we see "too many clicks" and "crowded layout." Can you see that these complaints are contradictory? This shows that designing websites in 2001 was as much an art as a science, and this is still true today. Design is not something that can be done blindly; we need as much input from the audience as possible. Chapter 7 discussed analytical modeling, which is a key technique for improving our Web designs. In addition, Chapter 4 introduced the idea of usability research, as well as experiments. In this chapter, we consider the audience to be tested.

Table 9.1 Complaints about websites ordered by frequency

Complaint	Percentage
Dead links	60
Slow to load	54
Need plug-in	35
Site times out	33
Bad link names	31
Too many clicks	28
Crowded layout	24
No skip button	22
No search button	20
Confusing layout	20

Source: Jupiter Media Metrix (2001).

While most of this chapter and the following chapters on design (10, 11, 12 and 13) will focus on websites, the message in these chapters is also applicable to social media and to mobile applications. With social media, the firm is at the mercy of the social platform manager; in most cases that would be Facebook. This means that the lessons of this string of chapters are harder to apply due to constraints imposed by Facebook as they control the overall look and feel of a group page or business page. Likewise, with mobile apps, the lessons of these chapters are also relevant but harder to apply due to the strictly limited screen real estate on the output side, and minimal keyboard and questionable voice processing available on the input side.

In addition to consumer input, external constraints, and screen real estate, we must consider the overall business and marketing goals of our site. Here we reintroduce the three contexts of online marketing provided in Chapter 1. Often the main role of a business website is either communication, selling or enabling connections. Communication refers to using digital media for the purposes of promotion or advertising. Compared to mass media, online media are ideal for establishing relationships with consumers. In this context, selling refers to using digital channels for retail. Finally, some firms like eBay use Internet Protocol (IP) networks to create exchange between groups of users. To pick another example, Amazon connects those who want to find a good book to those who want to write a review about a book they have already read. This makes both groups happier; the review writers get a built-in audience and the book buyers get some advice as to what they should buy. What is important now, however, is that how you design your app, your link, your page, or your entire site will depend on which of these three goals – communication, selling or connecting – is primary.

Given that you are clear on the goal, another key question concerns the site metric or objective (function) that can be used to assess your efforts. How will you know if you are far or near from your goal? How will you measure progress toward your goal? For communications sites we might think in terms of page views or time on site. For selling sites we might think in terms of unit or dollar sales. Finally, for sites that connect two or more groups, we might count the number or dollar amount of transactions exchanged between the two groups. eBay, for example, takes a certain percentage of each sale executed on the eBay platform.

Once we know our goal and how we plan to measure success, the next question that naturally occurs is, who is the target market or markets? Answering this question is the main focus of this chapter. Who is the "visitor" to the site? Who will be using this app? Who will be in the social network of your company? What are the benefits they seek? Are they look-ing for entertainment and enjoyment, or are they looking for information and learning? Are they trying to execute a transaction? Transactions will be covered in a later chapter. For now, we consider the difference between those who are simply seeking entertainment, and those who want to learn something. We call the first group "hedonic surfers," and the second group "utilitarian seekers."

Audience segmentation

Hirschman and Holbrook (1982) introduced the notion of utilitarian vs hedonic value with respect to shopping. Extending their discussion to elec-tronic interfaces, we might describe utilitarian searchers as those for whom the use of the site is rational or instrumental. In other words, the site is not an end in itself, but an instrument used to achieve some other goal. These folks have a work mentality and a goal orientation, and the goal is to find specific information.

Hedonic surfers, on the other hand, experience the site like a movie, or a sporting event. In the case of surfers, the site is an end in itself. This group is less directed and more exploratory. Their goal is to become immersed in the site, seeking symbolic, non-verbal, escapist elements. There are two types of hedonic experience (Hassenzahl, 2004): stimulation and identification. Stimulation requires vividness and novelty and typically some sort of chal-lenge (think video game), while identification includes self-expression or self-presentation (think Facebook or MySpace).

In the language of Chapter 2, where we discussed costs and benefits in terms of gives and gets, the gets are different for utilitarian searchers as compared to hedonic surfers. Given these differences between utilitarian searchers and hedonic surfers, we might ask what type of site works best? There is no single best answer here as each group is looking for something different. The searchers want a well-organized, logical, stripped down, fast site. The site should be transparent – it should stay out of the way while the searcher performs his or her task. Surfers, on the other hand, want a site that is interesting, novel, unique, entertaining, visual, complex. The site itself represents their focus.

If you have done a good job matching site characteristics to the benefits sought by the visitors to the site, your visitors may enter the "flow state," considered a key goal for interface design. We now turn to that topic.

Flow

Figure 9.1 The flow zone – hitting a match between skill and challenge

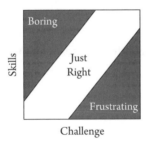

Flow is an important goal for firms communicating with an active user. According to Hoffman and Novak (1996):

> Flow is an optimal psychological experience occurring when there is a match between the challenge at hand and one's skills.

The match between challenge and skills is illustrated in Figure 9.1. The flow zone is situated in the middle, and labeled "Just Right." Too much skill for the challenge leads to boredom, while too little skill, in comparison to the amount needed, leaves the participant frustrated.

To create the flow state, it is generally necessary that the online experience includes concrete goals with immediate feedback as to movement towards or away from those goals. Flow typically involves some sort of distinction from everyday reality. A classic example occurs in sports, where our team uniform signifies that we are not acting within the confines of everyday reality.

In Chapter 1, we learned that the Internet is an interactive medium, and interactivity and user control are key antecedents of flow. The word "interactivity" is surprisingly hard to define, but let us, after Liu and Shrum (2002), note that interactivity includes the following properties:

● contingency – implies that current actions depend on previous actions;
● control – implies an active user is directing his or her online experience;
● feedback – implies two-way (or more) communications; and
● synchronicity – implies real-time responsiveness.

Interactivity can occur between two or more persons, between a person and message content or between a person and the medium or format (Liu and Shrum, 2002).

If the site can induce a flow state in visitors, we see a variety of effects (Williams and Dargel, 2004). Action and awareness merge in the mind of the visitor, and the visitor has a high level of concentration and involvement. There is a sense of play, of fun, and the visitor may experience time distortion and a loss of self-consciousness. We might characterize these effects by describing them as enhanced engagement. The long-term consequences of flow are beneficial for the firm, and explain why flow is considered so important (Hoffman and Novak, 1996). These long-term consequences include better memory for what happened, more exploration and participation, and perception of the activity as intrinsically motivating – that is, enjoyable in and of itself.

Let us review the difference between the utilitarian searcher and the hedonic surfer. For each group, what creates flow? For the searcher, it is the information itself, the task facing that searcher. On the other hand, for the surfer, flow is induced by the site, the symbols, the images, or video. For the surfer, flow comes not from an external task, but from experiencing the site. Rather than make the site disappear as we might want to do for searchers, we might wish to increase the site challenge to avoid boredom on the part of the surfer. Obviously, these goals are not completely compatible. This makes site design as much an art as a science.

 QUESTIONS AND EXERCISES

1   What are the implications of flow for websites engaged in communicating or promoting a brand? What about for retail websites that are selling something online?
2   Look at the following sites and try to judge whether they are appealing to utilitarian or hedonic values:
   (a)   www.ford.com;
   (b)   www.energizer.com;
   (c)   news.google.com;
   (d)   www.capitalhealth.com;
   (e)   Your university's home page.
3   Compare the following in terms of the level of interactivity: radio, a mapping app for your phone, your university website, a novel by the author Danielle Steel.
4   In this chapter the audience is divided into hedonic and utilitarian segments. There is an implicit assumption that we are talking about nations with high gross domestic products. Do you think that audiences in emerging nations in South America, Africa and Asia are similar or different than the audience in, let's say, North America or Europe?
5   In contrast to flow, other experts (Van Laer and de Ruyter, 2010) have proposed that transportation (described in Chapter 22) is critically important in the e-experience. Transportation occurs when a visitor consumes some content, like a story, and that content takes them into the story. When do you think transportation is more important than flow? When would flow be more important than transportation?

REFERENCES

Hassenzahl, M. (2004), "The interplay of beauty, goodness, and usability in interactive products," *Human–Computer Interaction*, **19** (4), 319–49.

Hirschman, E.C. and M.B. Holbrook (1982), "Hedonic consumption: Emerging concepts, methods and propositions," *Journal of Marketing*, **46** (3), 92–100.

Hoffman, D.L. and T.P. Novak (1996), "Marketing in hypermedia computer-mediated environments: Conceptual foundations," *Journal of Marketing*, **60** (3), 50–68.

Jupiter Media Metrix (2001), *Site Navigation: Differentiation and Customer Loyalty via Native Navigation*, June, 2001.

Kenkai (2007), "Website failure rate" [blog], accessed January 10, 2018 at http://www.kenkai.com/seo-blog-article-372.htm.

Liu, Y. and L.J. Shrum (2002), "What is interactivity and is it always such a good thing?" *Journal of Advertising*, **31** (4), 53–66.

McMillan, S.J. (2002), "Longevity of websites and interactive advertising communication," *Journal of Interactive Advertising*, **2** (2), 11–21.

Van Laer, T. and K. de Ruyter (2010), "In stories we trust: How narrative apologies provide cover for competitive vulnerability after integrity-violating blog posts," *International Journal of Research in Marketing*, **27** (2), 164–74.

Williams, R. and M. Dargel (2004), "From servicescape to 'cyberscape'," *Marketing Intelligence & Planning*, **22** (2/3), 310–20.

10

Human information processing

This chapter looks at the information we provide on the screen and describes how this information influences the consumer experience. This experience includes both costs and benefits, or in the language of Chapter 2, gives and gets. As we know, costs are not necessarily economic. The nature and amount of these costs partially depend on the three main sub-systems that exist in the mind, and the relative efficiency with which these three sub-systems are capable of processing app or website information. After presenting the three sub-systems, we will cover the steps that consumers go through, using these sub-systems in processing information.

Now we start with the names of these basic sub-systems of the human mind: sensory storage, short-term storage and long-term storage. These are pictured in Figure 10.1:

Figure 10.1 The human information processing system

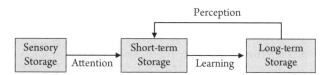

The figure shows that attention is the process by which information moves from the sensory storage to the mind's short-term storage system. Sensory storage holds information from the eye or the ear for a very short period of time (think about an afterimage). Short-term memory holds information for longer, but to keep that information in there, the consumer must constantly rehearse (think of repeating a phone number until you can get to your phone) or elaborate on it. The capacity of short-term storage is strictly limited to 7 ± 2 items. Thus, attention and the limited capacity of the short-term store comprise two critical bottlenecks in human information processing.

Learning is the process by which information moves from short-term storage to long-term storage. Typically, brute force repetition is not very effective at this task; it is necessary that the information be processed, or elaborated on, at the level of the meaning of the information. That process can be somewhat slow. Once information makes it to long-term storage, however, it can be held indefinitely. It appears that there is no limit to how much information can actually be stored in the long-term storage system. It is true, however, that acquiring new information in long-term storage can interfere with retrieval of older information.

Perception is the process by which information in long-term storage provides meaning for information in short-term storage via the relatively effortless process of recognition. Perception works via a network of connections or associations that exist in long-term storage. These connections provide meaning or context for the information stored there. In addition to perception, information in long-term storage can also be voluntarily recalled or remembered back into the short-term store.

What happens when a consumer lands on one of your pages or calls up your app? Assuming we want the information that appears on that page to have a maximum impact on the consumer, we need to carefully analyze what happens to that information in the mind of that consumer. We decompose the flow of that information in the mind of the consumer following the five-stage sequence presented by McGuire (1968). These stages are:

1. exposure;
2. attention;
3. comprehension and perception;
4. yielding and acceptance; and
5. retention.

These stages occur in the context of sensory storage, short-term storage and long-term storage. We now proceed through these five stages one by one, noting how digital marketers can utilize knowledge of each stage to facilitate the marketing goals of the site. At the end of this chapter, we will combine the stages to talk about the overall way that consumers look for information on a site, a process known as information foraging.

Exposure

The way to think of each of McGuire's five stages is as a series of gateways. If the consumer does not pass through all these gateways, the information on your page is basically lost. The first gateway is exposure. If the consumer is not exposed to the information on your page, that information does not pass through the first gateway. It has to be in front of the visitors' eyeballs or otherwise they will not react to it.

Attention

Attention is one of the key bottlenecks of the human mind, primarily because the short-term store can only deal with a small amount of information at once. By definition, attention consists of the reading out of information from the sensory store into short-term memory. Typically, a very small percentage of information on a web page is read out of the sensory store and into short-term storage.

Hong, Thong and Tam (2007) highlight the distinction between voluntary and involuntary attention. The user's goals and intentions drive the former, and depends on the customer's anticipation of where to look in the visual field to find a specific search target. This form of attention can be primed or cued and is subject to expectation. In other words, if you don't expect to see something, you don't see it (this happens while driving, for example). We can think of voluntary attention as being a top-down process guided by what the visitor is trying to do and what they expect to see. Involuntary attention is different. Physical factors, such as size, intensity, color, motion, attractive stimuli and spatial arrangement, impact involuntary attention. These factors grab attention without planning on the part of the visitor and act via bottom-up processes. Involuntary attention is effortless, but voluntary attention takes some effort on the part of the user and so can be counted as a cognitive cost.

It is possible to change behavior in the absence of attention though a technique known as priming. Consumer reaction can be primed with advertisements and images in a way that does not explicitly involve the short-term storage system. Such reactions have at least been demonstrated in laboratory experiments (see, e.g., Stevenson, Bruner and Kumar, 2000).

Comprehension and perception

By definition, perception consists of the contact between information in long-term storage and short-term storage. For example, if I see the letters UN on a web page, the meaning of that acronym is stored in long-term storage, and I therefore comprehend it.

Of course, previous learning comes into play in comprehension or perception. Most learning is cultural in nature; that is, what we learn depends on our social environment. In America, we learn that mailboxes are in front of a house and look like rounded tubes of aluminum. In Italy, we learn that mailboxes are on main streets, are in the shape of a box, and are red. Because people have to learn how to identify objects on the screen, the symbols and metaphors that we use must match the culture of the intended audience.

Note that many of the common objects that appear on app displays or web pages, like a shopping cart, or the very notion of "checkout," depend on consumers' offline cultural experiences to function. Interaction designers can use metaphors to enable comprehension. A well-chosen metaphor brings the consumer along effortlessly.

Yielding and acceptance

There are two main "routes" that end in yielding and acceptance. These are discussed in more detail in Chapter 14. For now, note that these two routes are known as the central and peripheral routes to persuasion. The central route is based on logic and assumes elaboration, which is another name for processing in short-term storage. The peripheral route is based on emotion, and assumes little elaboration.

Retention

The ability of the consumer to remember what is seen on pages depends on many factors. Despite what some might believe, the least effective method of inducing retention is simple repetition, unless those repetitions are spread out in time. In general, we know that spacing in time between exposures of the same information leads to better memory than massed repetition. Memory is better when the consumer is forced to actively retrieve information, as compared to when the consumer merely passively reads the information. Similarly, elaboration or thinking about information tends to create better memories for that information. Of course, thinking and elaboration take cognitive effort.

There are a lot of cognitive costs involved in consumer information processing. Attention is limited and voluntary attention in particular takes effort. Reading also takes real cognitive effort, as does elaboration or even simply holding information in short-term storage. With respect to long-term storage, learning is fairly slow and generally requires effort, and in the other direction, willful recall from long-term storage is also effortful. Perhaps the only low-cost cognitive processes described above are involuntary attention and perception. The rest represent greater costs. When you add in time and opportunity costs, we can understand that the consumer is doing us a favor

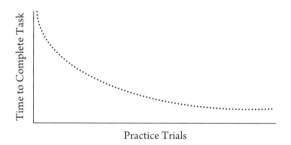

Figure 10.2 The Law of Practice. After Murray and Häubl (2003)

by staying on our website or using our app. It is up to us not to waste that favor.

If the consumer returns to the website, they may be able to remember what they learned previously, making them more efficient. Comprehension can take place with a relatively low amount of cognitive effort. This can serve to lock in a competitive advantage because at that point the consumer may not wish to switch to a new site and begin the learning process there. Figure 10.2 is a representation of the Law of Practice from a paper by Murray and Häubl (2007).

As you can see, the Law of Practice states that time to complete a task drops rapidly with practice as the learner develops a particular set of skills. If the consumer gets skilled in working your site, and this skill does not transfer easily to competitor sites, this adds a switching cost and makes that consumer more likely to repatronize your service.

Information foraging

The theory of information foraging makes the assumption that a person looking for information is trying to gain the most information for the least amount of effort, including the types of cognitive effort described above.

The theory is based on evolutionary biology. By analogy, if we contemplate a bear looking for berries, we understand that the bear has to decide if the bushes that it sees at a distance are worth the effort of walking over to them. Of course, if there are enough berries, the calories expended in the walk are less than the calories ingested from the berries. If the bear makes too many mistakes, burning more calories than consumed wandering around looking for berries, pretty soon it is "bye bye bear." Likewise, humans do not want to spend too much effort digging out information from our website. This means that our goal as online marketers is to convey the "richness" of our pages even at a distance. Conveying information at a distance is called conveying scent.

It is worth walking around this site! There are lots of berries! That is what scent is about. Now the meaning of what a "berry" is depends on whether the bear (the visitor) is a searcher or a surfer. The searcher asks whether the next click will take him or her closer to what he or she is looking for. The surfer wonders if the time is worth the enjoyment that might ensue as a result of the next click.

QUESTIONS AND EXERCISES

1 Discuss the notion of exposure in terms of desktop PCs, laptop PCs, tablets and smartphones. How should designers customize for these different devices?
2 Can you think of other metaphors that are used in Web navigation and website design? What symbols are used on your favorite sites to aid navigation?
3 If memory is better when the consumer actively retrieves information from memory, how might we design our online experience to encourage that? What tricks or techniques might we use to encourage visitors to recall what they previously saw on our site?
4 Think about a site you have visited recently. What can you remember about it? What sticks out in your mind?
5 Go to a website that is written in a language that you cannot comprehend. Can you figure out what is going on, and how and where you can navigate on the site? If you were able to understand at least part of the site, how were you able to do so? (No cheating by using Google translate!)

 REFERENCES

Hong, W., J.Y.L. Thong and K.Y. Tam (2007), "How do Web users respond to non-banner-ads animation? The effects of task type and user experience," *Journal of the American Society for Information Science and Technology*, **58** (10), 1467–82.

McGuire, W.J. (1968), "Personality and attitude change: An information-processing theory," in A.G. Greenwald, T.C. Brock and T.M. Ostrom (eds), *Psychological Foundations of Attitudes*, New York: Academic Press.

Murray, Kyle B. and Gerald Häubl (2003), "A human capital perspective of skill acquisition and interface loyalty," *Communications of the ACM*, **46** (12), 272–78.

Murray, Kyle B. and Gerald Häubl (2007), "Explaining cognitive lock-in: The role of skill-based habits of use in consumer choice," *Journal of Consumer Research*, **34** (1), 77–88.

Stevenson, J.S., G.C. Bruner II and A. Kumar (2000), "Webpage background and viewer attitudes," *Journal of Advertising Research*, **40** (1/2), 29–34.

11

Visual design practice

> We made the buttons on the screen look so good you'll want to lick them.
>
> (Steve Jobs)

In his typically fanatical way, in this quote Steve Jobs informs us just how important visual design is. Overall, the design of a website takes place at three distinct levels. There are important design decisions to be made at the lowest level of individual page components, such as link wording, text and visual elements including art, buttons and other images. A second level deals with the overall structure of the page and a third, higher level is concerned with the way that pages connect to each other. This chapter on the visual look and feel of the pages of a website relates mostly to the first and second levels. The chapter is also relevant to the smaller screens that are available to phone and tablet users.

Let us review at this point the "big three" contexts for digital marketing. One might wish to design a page to communicate with the customer, especially to enhance the customer–firm relationship. A second context might occur when the goal is to have the customer execute a transaction on the site – that is, persuade the customer to purchase one or more items on the site. Finally, a third page design context occurs when the site's goal is connecting people or firms – for example, eBay (sellers and buyers) or Google (site owners and site seekers). Each of these three contexts will have different possible objective functions (see Chapter 7), whether those be time on site or return visits (communicating), sales volume (selling), or exchanges made (connecting). In all three cases, however, moving towards the objective will depend on the quality of visual design. In addition to the objective functions of design, the branding of the site comes into play as well.

In our goal to create a well-designed site, the chess board, or the battle ground, is the consumer's screen. Since military analogies in marketing are overused, we should change the analogy from war to ecology. You can think of the screen in front of the consumer as being like a forest or a meadow. The consumer has given you part or all of some visual display. The screen real estate they give you is valuable and should never be wasted! Like a flower in a meadow, your pages must attract that consumer.

The size of the screen they have granted us is traditionally measured in pixels (picture elements, or dots). The number of pixels available, the real estate, varies greatly out in the market, as does the number of pixels per inch (ppi). Another factor to consider is how far from the eye the device is held. Here are some example sizes, with the number of column pixels given first, then the number of rows:

- Dell 2407WFP 1920 × 1200 (108 ppi – desktop monitor);
- ASUS PB287Q 3840 × 2160 (157 ppi – desktop monitor);
- Samsung Note 4 1440 × 2560 (515 ppi – mobile phone); and
- Google Nexus 7 1200 × 1920 (323 ppi – tablet).

So, we don't know beforehand how big the screen is, how many pixels it contains and how far from the eye it will be. Of course, they may have only given you part of their display, which adds another unknown. If you include older models, like the 640 × 960 pixels of the iPhone 4, even more flexibility is needed. Pages must look good on a variety of screen sizes, and this requires we should utilize the principle of modularity. Content should be separate from format. Generally, the software closest to the user (the end-to-end principle from Chapter 3) is best positioned to figure out how to present the information to that user, which is to say to figure out the format for the content. Fortunately, this principle is part of the philosophy of the Hypertext Markup Language (HTML). HTML is part of the Hypertext Transfer Protocol (HTTP), proposed originally by Tim Berners-Lee in 1989.

Visual design for the Web

Those pixels we have been granted must do two jobs: provide navigation and display the actual page content. Often this dual-purpose problem is solved using one of the following two schemes. The first scheme is known as Navigation Bar and Body. Here part of the page is given over to navigational links, while the main part shows the content. This should sound familiar to many students since numerous sites use this approach. Figure 11.1 is a screen shot of Amazon, showing several navigation bars.

A second scheme might be called Banner and Menu. In this plan, the top of the page shows a logo, banner or perhaps flash movie of some kind, while the main body of the page located beneath the banner contains one or more

Figure 11.1 Visual Web design following the "Navigation Bar and Body" approach

sets of bulleted menu items. The Florida State University (FSU) College of Business home page, among many others, shown in Figure 11.2, uses this basic concept.

Using either of these schemes is not easy, since the human eye expects visual displays of all kind to be balanced or symmetric. The notion of visual balance informs us that the weight appearing in each of the four quadrants of a screen should be approximately equal. Neither Banner and Menu nor Navigation Bar and Body divide up the screen equally in terms of space, so the items appearing in the four quadrants must balance in terms of their overall perceptual weight – that is, how visually "strong" they appear.

Designing pages can be facilitated by creating a layout grid. Each type of page might have a different layout grid. For each of these, you decide how you will divide up the screen into sections. The grid serves as a template so that all pages on your site that have a similar function look the same. A hypothetical layout grid appears in Figure 11.3. A related technique is to create a wireframe, also known as an interaction map. The idea here is to map out the possible navigation sequences of the user by showing which

Figure 11.2 Visual Web design following the "Banner and Menu" approach

Figure 11.3 An example layout grid

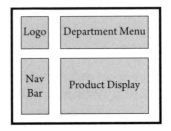

screen is connected to which other screen. A simple example can be seen in Figure 11.4.

Of course, an attractive layout takes as much artistic instinct as it does marketing knowledge. I might emphasize this by referring to a different medium – namely, music. Claude Debussy once said that, "music is the space between the notes." Likewise, in page design, notice the white space and look to see if it is pleasing. Of course, master musicians like Debussy, as well as master site designers, can afford to break the rules. But rule-breaking requires that you know those rules very well.

Figure 11.4 An example of a wireframe

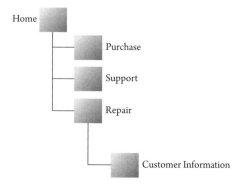

Figure 11.5 Two examples of mobile visual design: circles versus cards

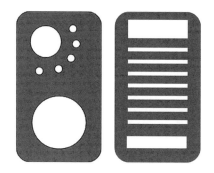

Two sample app design schemes

In principle, app design is not so different from Web design, except with a smaller screen. Two general categories of design have emerged: a circular design that utilizes clusters of related commands or options and a rectangular design that organizes options or content horizontally (Figure 11.5). One of the ways in which a rectangular approach is used is to facilitate cards, which employ the metaphor of the index card for notifications and other purposes.

App design is further complicated by the fact that the user can change the orientation from vertical (portrait) to horizontal (landscape). In addition to the challenges of dealing with smartphones and tablets, marketers also need to think about other devices, including game consoles, watches and various other interfaces that are emerging as part of the Internet of Things (IoT). The consumer lives in a multiscreen world and we must adapt.

Summary

Following the principles of consumer information processing we learned in Chapter 10, we should make sure our visual design does not create needless cognitive costs on the part of the visitors. In terms of exposure, if the design layout is too wide or long for the screen, it is clear that visitors might not see that part of the design. The overall layout and the use of artistic or visual elements within it should also be chosen considering the attention of the visitor. The involuntary attention system is particularly sensitive to movement and to color contrast. Since the attention system is so limited, your page layout must emphasize one or two priorities for the page at the expense of the other elements. The voluntary attention system allows visitors to scan for the information they are seeking. Typically, eye scanning of a screen occurs in an F pattern (Pernice, 2017).

Comprehension is another key consideration from Chapter 10. Images and other visual design elements need to be chosen that will be understood by the audience. This means that the designer must be familiar with the culture of that audience. Since it is difficult to learn new information, Web visitors often rely on link colors to remind themselves of what pages they have already visited. HTML generally allows you to distinguish between visited links (the default color is purple) and non-visited links (that default to blue). These link colors have been learned well by Web users and are changed at your peril!

In wrapping up the chapter, we return to the point that the visual design of a site must consider branding – the colors, fonts, graphical elements and writing style on a site must conform to your branding aesthetic and communications strategy. In addition, the visual cues on a site create an emotional atmosphere that needs to be conducive to your branding goals. All the specific visual elements have to contribute to the overall gestalt of the site – its total look and feel. Certainly, a site visited mostly by hedonic surfers will need to have a different atmosphere than one frequented by utilitarian searchers (see Chapter 9). What brand values are you trying to convey? We might wish to communicate one of the following: efficiency, competence, fun, high technology, empathy, coolness, safety or happiness. What's more, the same values have to emerge on any size of screen or type of device that the consumer is using. It should be clear that getting visual design to work well is not at all easy, and in fact calls for a triple skill set: artistic, technology and marketing.

? QUESTIONS AND EXERCISES

1 Be prepared to give the URL of a home page that you think is particularly attractive from a visual point of view, and also a URL of a home page that you think is particularly ugly from a visual point of view. Describe what you like about it, or in the case of the ugly page, what you don't like about it.

2 Given the contents of this chapter, as well as previous chapters on design theory, what might be some Dos and Don'ts for Web page design?

3 How can we balance a navigation bar with the rest of the screen?

4 Pick the website for a well-known brand and look to see how the visual elements of the site enhance or match the brand. How is (or isn't) the website consistent with other aspects of the branding approach or the brand personality?

5 Discuss using visual elements for branding in social media. What restrictions to visual design exist in social media that are not present on a website?

6 There are two recent competing schools of thought for digital visual design. One is skeuomorphism and the other is known as flat design. Go on the Internet and find the definitions of these two approaches and three typical examples of each. Be sure to cite the sources of your definitions and examples.

7 Voice interfaces are becoming more common. We have Siri, OK Google, Cortana and Alexa, among others. What would we need to add to this chapter to include a section on "voice design"?

 REFERENCE

Pernice, K. (2017), "F-shaped pattern for reading on the Web: Misunderstood, but still relevant (even on mobile)," *Nielsen Norman Group*, accessed January 11, 2018 at http://www.useit.com/alertbox/reading_pattern.html.

12

Writing for the screen

This second chapter on owned media will continue to concentrate on the Web, specifically on writing. Despite the concentration on the Web, I will point out that anything true about writing for a computer screen is even truer when writing for smaller screens like those on smartphones or tablets (there is more on these devices in Chapter 18).

So, in Chapter 11 we noted that Web design takes place at three levels: individual page components, text and visual elements; the level of the entire page; and the highest level that specifies how the pages interconnect. In this chapter, the focus is on writing, which comes into play at the level of individual page text – that is, the text we put on each page and the words we use for our links.

The best way to think about writing for the Web, as well as for mobile, is to think about how not to write for the Web! There are two basic rules to keep in mind here: (1) the Web is not TV; and (2) a computer screen is not paper.

After comparing television and print to the Web, we talk about how much material to put on each page. As you will see below, modularizing content is an important Web technique. We finish the chapter with some hopefully well-chosen words on link wording. But we start the chapter by comparing the Web to TV.

The Web vs television

Many of us are used to seeing ads on mass media like TV and we implicitly think that TV ads are the prototype, or ideal type, of advertising. In fact, online promotion is different than mass media promotion. On television, the goal of the advertiser is to get the attention of the viewer, who is, after all, trying to watch a show. In this case, we must cut through the background noise. Fundamentally, we are intruding on the viewer's activity.

In contrast, in Chapter 1 we learned that the Internet is a user-driven medium. On the Web, the visitor, who is in charge, has already come to you. You don't have to shout at them. Visitors are presumably already motivated to hear your message. Your ad copy should therefore be more factual, more cognitive and less emotional (Nielsen, 2000). To put this another way, the central route to persuasion makes a lot of sense online. Nor do we want to engage in hard sell, or talk down to the visitor.

Since the user is in charge on the Web, the user has control over where he or she enters the site and the order of pages he or she reads. We can thus conclude that the Web is generally not a serial medium like a book or a television show. Since the user can enter your site at any sub-page, each page needs to be self-contained with links to any preliminary, fundamental material and to have hooks into the overall navigation scheme. We can call a page with only incoming links a dead-end page and note that it does not contribute to the marketing goals of the site.

The Web vs paper

Ah, paper! Invented by the Egyptians around 3500 BC, improved by the Chinese around 100 AD, this stuff is always maligned by true computer geeks. But paper is actually pretty impressive technology. You really can call it technology. Paper, in fact, is a very high-resolution output medium, which makes it easy to read and comprehend. It is becoming a more interactive medium due to QR codes, which are the square digital symbols readable by mobile phones (discussed further in Chapter 18). The one negative thing we can say about it, and it is a fairly big negative, is that it is expensive. It is expensive because it is "write once" technology that takes up a lot more space than disk storage.

Computer storage, on the other hand, is quite cheap. Since disk storage is so cheap, it makes sense to include lots of extra information on the website, things that you couldn't afford to print, or to mail or store in paper form. Ideal online textual material can include glossaries, lists, histories, bibliographies, instructions, details, tips and technical specifications.

But now we come to the downside of computer displays. Digital screens generally lack the resolution, or size, of paper. This is something that the eye notices even if you are not consciously aware of it. The result is that readers struggle with long texts on a screen, compared to paper. The effort it takes to read on a screen is higher than on paper, while at the same time comprehension and memory are reduced (Jabr, 2013).

This suggests that we should be extremely concise when we write for the Web. What's more, the increased effort induces readers to skim text on a screen. Given that, it makes sense for us to facilitate skimming by using high-lighting, captions, color changes, bold text, or larger fonts for key text, along with bulleted lists. It is a good practice to highlight key phrases so that the Web visitor can quickly scan the page and grasp the most important com-munications points.

In addition, the visitor is likely scanning for links to click on. It is natural to combine the skimming advice given in the above paragraph with writing link anchor text. The underlining and blue font color that we see with links can be used to create a natural highlighting technique. Search engines such as Google also tend to use link anchor text to try to understand what is on the page. Generic link copy such as "Click here" is useless and should be avoided. Your link anchor text should provide the user with a clear notion of what they will see if they click on that link – that is, what the link payoff page is all about.

Anchor text provides scent (see Chapter 10) for the payoff page, but there are different types of payoffs. Some links are purely navigational in nature. The link is moving the visitor from one logical part of the site to another. Other sorts of links represent related or additional information. Your job as a writer of link anchor text is to let the visitor sense what is on the payoff page. In other words, your job is to provide scent – information at a distance. This is a hard job but don't give up on it and fail to create links! A page with no outbound links is called a dangling node. Perhaps a better term would be "dead end." If the user enters your site on such a page, they will probably just leave once they are done with it.

Earlier in this section we have seen that a dense page of text is painful to read online, so being concise makes sense. But what if you have lots of information to convey?

Modularization

If things get too long, modularize. According to Nielsen (2000), modulariza-tion is a key principle for writing on the Web. It allows you to unlock the power behind inexpensive disk storage, and to therefore leverage what the Web is better at than paper. A modular structure is consistent with the notion of the Internet as a user-driven (versus mass) medium as it puts the reader in charge. Consistent-sized modules help the user find the site's natural rhythm. What's more, modular nesting is ideal when information is hierarchical, a very common occurrence that we study in Chapter 13. Modules help you avoid forcing the user to scroll, so we know that at the very least they are exposed to your information if they arrive on the page. Modularization then suggests that we should keep the amount of content on any one web page modest. What about the links that are on a page? Let's address that question now.

How many links to include on each page?

In general, modularization motivates us to have relatively small pages with just a few links each. But to further guide us in the "how big should this page be" decision, contemplate the following two laws, which can be called the Total Click Law and the Link Cannibalism Law.

Consider two pages such that page i has a superset of the links that appear on page j. In other words, page i has the same links as page j, and then at least one more. Define T as the total clicks given by visitors to the entire page. The Total Click Law states that:

> If page i has a superset of the links that appear on page j, the total clicks on page i will be greater than or equal to the total clicks for page j.

We write this as:

$$T_i \geq T_j$$

where T_i represents the total number of clicks that accrue to page i.

The Link Cannibalism Law, on the other hand, deals with the clickthrough rate, call it C, of any one specific link. It states that:

> If page i has a superset of the links that appear on page j, the clickthrough for a particular link on page i will be less than or equal to the clickthrough for that link on page j.

Or, mathematically:

$$C_i \leq C_j$$

Here C_i is the number of clicks given to a specific link appearing on page i.

These two equations work in opposite directions, so this leaves us in a quandary. Would we prefer to have more clicks overall, or do we wish to emphasize a particular link and not create more "competition" for that link within the page? The answer will depend on what the overall site goal is and specifically on what the goal of the page is. For example, an e-tail site might want to funnel visitors towards any link that moves the visitor closer to executing a transaction. For the e-tailer, the Link Cannibalism Law is therefore paramount. A communications site might want to give the visitor as many reasons as possible to stay on the site to grow the relationship with them. The Total Click Law should be ascendant when the goal is to retain, extend or leverage relationships.

We now switch from questions pertaining to how much to put on a web page, to questions about the style of writing for the Web. Along with modules, another key idea for writing on the Web is the inverted pyramid writing style. Let's talk about that next.

Inverted pyramid writing style

As Jakob Nielsen (2000) notes, since many people do not scroll on a web page, it is important to put the conclusions at the beginning of the page. Such an approach is known as the inverted pyramid writing style and is typically used by journalists. One starts with the conclusions. Next, you expand to each of the main supporting points and finally you provide background information and details. This style goes well with bulleted lists and hierarchical information.

In conclusion, writing for the Web is totally unlike writing ad copy for a mass medium like TV, and it involves a radically different style from writing on paper. What this means is that if you think that lots of people are likely to print your site, you should have two versions: the Web version and a second, printer-friendly version.

? QUESTIONS AND EXERCISES

1 In this chapter we note that the Internet is not TV and the Web is not like paper plastered on a computer screen. So, assuming we now know what the online experience is not like, discuss what the online experience is like. Which media are like the Internet in at least some respects and why?

2 Pretend that you are creating a detailed blog entry that describes your typical Wednesday activities. Also pretend that you are going to link to the home page for this course. What would the link say, and what would the stuff around the link say, both leading up to it and following it. In other words, provide the link and its context.

3 What is the resolution of your phone? How many pixels per inch does it have? How does this compare to the number of dots per inch created by the printer you most often use?

4 Pick a hedonic product that you enjoy. This might be clothes, music, jewelry, cologne, automobiles, art, film, theater, travel, food, sports, recreation, games, books, or anything that is fun rather than useful. Assume you have at most 30 characters to describe the benefits of this product to a site visitor. Create a description of your brand in less than 30 characters.

5 In this exercise, pick a product that you find useful. This might be window cleaner, paper towels, blank DVDs, light bulbs, your local pharmacy, auto repair, a check cashing service, an online discount air travel site or anything that is useful rather than fun. Assume you have at most 30 characters to describe the benefits of this product to a site visitor.

6 Iambic pentameter is a common form in poetry. Lines of iambic pentameter consist of exactly ten syllables. A stanza of poetry often consists of four lines where either lines 1/2 and 3/4 rhyme, or 1/3 and 2/4 rhyme. Write a stanza of iambic pentameter extolling the virtues of any website of your choice. Hint: this exercise can really teach you how to economize words and focus on saying something succinctly.

 REFERENCES

Jabr, F. (2013), "Why the brain prefers paper," *Scientific American*, **309** (5), 48–53.

Nielsen, J. (2000), *Designing Web Usability*, Indianapolis: New Riders Publishing.

13

Site structure

From previous chapters, you will recall that the design of a site takes place on three levels. There is the level of the link – that is, the wording or images designed to induce a click. There is the level of the page or screen – that is, how to format the visual appearance of the screen and what content to put on the screen. Finally, we come to the level of the entire site or entire application program – that is, how the various pages or screens connect to each other.

Most of the discussion in this third chapter on owned media will focus on the Web. Mobile and tablet apps tend to be relatively simple, covering a minimal number of topics. On the other hand, we can think of all the topics that go on a website as often creating a fairly complex sort of "space." This space might imitate normal three-dimensional space in some ways or it might not, but in this chapter the concept of information space refers to the totality of information on a site and how it is connected.

Now any space worthy of the word space must have a way to measure distance between two points or nodes. In the case of the Web, the distance between the page I am on and some other page is the number of clicks required for me to go from the current page to that other page. If we define a page as a node, and the presence of a hypertext link between two pages as a connection, we can see that an information space is a type of network. Within this network we travel between nodes by clicking.

We now explore the nature of different categories of information spaces, how they are represented to the user and how the user would move within them. In this, we recognize the need of the site visitor to gain an intuition for the structure of network that constitutes the site. The visitor needs to know the answer to three questions, which have been paraphrased from Nielsen (2000):

- Where am I now?
- Where have I been?
- How do I get to where I want to go?

To answer these three questions, the visitor tries to pick up scent (information foraging is discussed in Chapter 10). The visitor needs to develop a mental model of the information space, internalizing the "lay of the land" so to speak. Of course, compounding the difficulty of the task is the fact that the visitor may enter the site at any page.

We next cover some prototypical examples of information space design. These are more or less pure types, and most websites represent a mixture of these types. Nevertheless, the following four categories will help us understand the possibilities: linear-sequential, hierarchical, faceted and semantic information spaces.

Linear-sequential information spaces

Figure 13.1 A representation of a linear information space

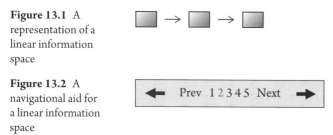

Figure 13.2 A navigational aid for a linear information space

A linear-sequential structure is ideal for converting paper documents to the Web, for storytelling or narrative, for making a logical presentation, or explaining procedures. A schematic diagram of such a structure appears in Figure 13.1.

The little rectangles represent pages and the arrows show the direction of the hypertext links. Navigational movement tends to be "left–right" in linear-sequential navigation spaces, or perhaps we could describe this as "forwards–backwards." The navigational aids and the URLs employed by the site can help the visitor understand the big three questions above (Where am I now? Where have I been? How do I get to where I want to go?) if they are chosen to logically reflect the sequential nature of the site. For URLs, one simple plan is to include a number as part of the page name. A classic nav bar as might be used on a linear site is shown in Figure 13.2. Note that the user is currently on page 2, so that the "2" is "grayed out" and cannot be clicked.

Hierarchical information spaces

Hierarchical information spaces have a tree-like structure, meaning that there is a main menu, and each item on the main menu may itself have

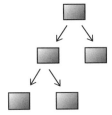

Figure 13.3 A representation of a hierarchical information space

a menu of other items (Figure 13.3). Classical computer menus always looked like this back in the day. Also, disk folder structure still tends to be hierarchical. While the word classical might imply "old-fashioned," such menus are still ideal for searchers who wish to drill down. The use of the expression "drill down" gives us a clue to the fact that movement in a hierarchy tends to be "up–down." Visual navigational tools as well as URLs should reflect the hierarchical nature of the site. URLs can utilize folders or directories that reflect hierarchies, for example: /products/flowers/roses.

Nav bars used for hierarchies are sometimes referred to as breadcrumb trails. An example appears in Figure 13.4. In the example, we are viewing a page called Detail, which is within the "Sub" category, which is itself nested within "Main," which is nested in turn under the "Top" page. There are hypertext links to Top, Main and Sub.

Figure 13.4 A navigational aid for a hierarchical information space

Top: Main: Sub: Detail

Faceted information spaces

A faceted (or factorial) information space design (Figure 13.5) combines two different factors – for example, product family (super, regular and budget) and model (left-handed, right-handed and ambidextrous). Each model might be somewhat different for each product family, and each model for each product family could have its own page. In effect, the information space resembles a spreadsheet and looks like a table of some kind with both rows and columns, and possibly additional dimensions (tiers). Facets are dimensions or characteristics of the information being classified (La Barre, 2004), and values are realizations of a facet. Facets are much like built-in tags for a page that can guide navigation to that page. A university might be public or private, so in this example the facet is "source of funding" and the values are simply either "public" or "private." Unlike a standard table, in facet theory not all value combinations need exist. So, for example, two

Figure 13.5 A representation of a faceted information space
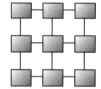

facets of wine might be color (red, rose, white) and location (California, Chile, Australia, France), and our store might not offer any Chilean reds, just whites.

In a faceted information space, movement can be either up–down or left–right. In other words, we can move between facets or within facets. Staying with our wine example, we could explore all the red wines, regardless of provenance, or we could change facets and decide to explore all the wines from France. E-tail websites often structure the products they sell with brand name as one facet and with various product attributes functioning as other facets.

Semantic information spaces

In a semantic information space, any two nodes might be linked (Figure 13.6). Here we might leverage the natural or logical connections in our information to create paths between related pages. Such a structure tends to enhance exploration and learning and is ideal for hedonistic surfers. Semantic information spaces are a very natural model for hypertext. Wikis, in particular, utilize this type of network space, connecting related encyclopedia entries with hyperlinks. In addition to sites based on the Wikipedia model, any site that allows user tagging tends to generate links based on the natural connections between tagged objects (like photos), to the linked or referred entities (friends).

It is sometimes the case that semantic information spaces encourage search-centric navigation. An effective within-site search box is therefore a must for semantic information spaces. This can be compared to hierarchical

Figure 13.6 A representation of a semantic information space
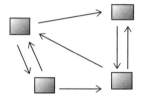

information spaces, which tend to encourage visitors, as has been mentioned, to "drill" down through the menu.

An overview of interaction design

Ideal Web design conveys overall site structure so that visitors can easily understand how each page fits into the information space, and they can develop an intuition about pages they have not seen. This intuition – call it a mental model – creates scent for the visitor, allowing expectations about the pages of the site not immediately in view. Links are worded so that the visitor has a sense of where that link will take them. Pages are constructed so that the visitor can easily understand what they are about by skimming or scanning. Navigation aids or page names convey the way in which pages are connected.

The task of executing good design at all three levels – the level of the link, the level of the whole page and the structure of the entire site – is a difficult one. Recall that two of the concepts introduced in Chapter 4 are usability testing and active experimentation. It should be re-emphasized that there are many unknowns to site design, which in effect is more of an art than a science. The implication is that we must subject our designs to usability testing and active experimentation to see what works, what is confusing, and what satisfies.

Good website design not only involves designing a website. One must also perform the less glamorous tasks involved in site maintenance. Such tasks include watching for common errors in the Web log (see Chapter 4), monitoring product and price changes, keeping the content fresh or up to date, constantly testing for, and then pruning dead links, monitoring and adapting to Web log data patterns, listening to and reacting to customer feedback and benchmarking versus the competition.

 QUESTIONS AND EXERCISES

1 What sort of structure would you use to represent a site selling gardening tools? How about a site selling bikes?

2 Describe how a jewelry retailer might use a faceted structure to describe his or her inventory.

3 Describe how a foreign language textbook author might use a networked information space to create a website to facilitate learning foreign words.

4 Imagine you have a website where the critical goal is to get visitors to donate to a community center. What site structure would be ideal for this? If the chapter does not include the ideal structure, sketch it out on a piece of paper or on a slide presentation program.

5 Describe the information space for YouTube and compare it to Flickr. How are the spaces of those sites designed? Are they equally effective?

REFERENCES

La Barre, K. (2004), "The use of faceted analytico-synthetic theory as revealed in the practice of website construction and design," unpublished doctoral dissertation, University of Indiana, accessed January 10, 2018 at https://mafiadoc.com/the-use-of-faceted-analytico-synthetic-_59f7463f1723dda6ae97f09f.html.

Nielsen, J. (2000), *Designing Web Usability*, Indianapolis, IN: New Riders Publishing.

14

Interactive advertising

The focus of this chapter is "advertising" or paid media. Numerous chapters in this book have been about advertising in some sense, but the focus of this chapter is somewhat different. Advertising is an impersonal form of promotion that in general, at least in the past, has tended to involve relatively intrusive communication with little user control and only one-directional communication flow. In that, we can compare this chapter to the thrust of two previous chapters (specifically, Chapters 7 and 8) that have dealt with the Internet's capability to build relationships, which in contrast requires two-way communication or interactivity. Despite this important difference between e-advertising and classical advertising, we ought to go back and see what traditional advertising can teach us about advertising on digital networks. We start this review by contemplating three potential goals of advertising and then two different routes we might take to achieving persuasion.

Thinking, feeling or doing

So, first let us take a step back and begin by talking about advertising in general. Advertising needs to be carefully coordinated with other forms of communication – a point of view known as integrated marketing communication or IMC (see below). Traditionally, advertising tends to take on one of three possible goals: cognition, affect or behavior. Cognition pertains to awareness, knowledge or mindshare and advertising can have as its goal to try to change cognition in favor of the advertised brand. The goal here might be to establish the brand at the front of the mind, or it might involve beliefs about the brand's attributes. Affect refers to emotion, and sometimes it is the goal of advertising to establish or change emotional responses such as attitude, image or liking. Behavior represents a third possible goal. We may advertise to increase the probability of trial, the probability of repurchase, to increase the volume of repurchasing, to generate positive word-of-mouth, or to up-sell or cross-sell.

Two routes to persuasion

How do ads impact cognition, affect and behavior? There are two general tactics we might use (Petty, Cacioppo and Schumann, 1983). The first tactic is known as the central route to persuasion. When we use the central route, our plan is to effect attitude change based on the consumer's purposeful evaluation, logic or "elaboration" (see Chapter 10). In other words, we want the consumer to think about our message and accept its logic. The central route can produce very long-lasting and enduring attitudes that directly influence the consumer's intention to purchase. The central route is most effective when the consumer is willing and able to elaborate on or think about our arguments. Such a condition occurs when the consumer is involved, interested and motivated, as might happen during extended problem solving (a topic in Chapter 15). The central route goes hand in hand with a very detailed website that could appeal to a utilitarian searcher.

The second tactic is known as the peripheral route to persuasion. Rather than use logic and rely on consumer elaboration, the logic in this route is minimal or non-existent. Instead, an advertisement working the peripheral route might rely on the attractiveness of the spokesperson. A peripheral advertisement might simply try to include many arguments, or more likely, use a beautiful scene with beautiful music, showing beautiful people being happy together. When a peripheral route ad succeeds, it tends to happen relatively quickly. The effectiveness of such an ad depends on the mood state of the consumer and their emotional situation. Peripheral persuasion can even occur by means of a banner ad that was not clicked, just viewed. The peripheral route would seem to be ideal for a website that appeals to the hedonic surfer.

Types of electronic marketing communications

Next, let's review the various sorts of marketing communications media. Below is a partial list of advertising formats:

Here we have some classic offline advertising:

- **Broadcast TV and radio spots:** These might include the 15-second or 30-second spots that are familiar to all. TV, and especially radio, are increasingly being distributed over Internet Protocol (IP) networks but for now we will still categorize them as non-digital.
- **Product placement:** This tactic is becoming more popular and often gives the appearance of accident or coincidence rather than purposeful

advertisement. When brand logos show up in movies or other performances there is often nothing accidental about it.

- **Sponsorship:** Here we have a relatively long-term relationship between the advertiser and a third party. Stadiums, events and other phenomena can be sponsored. It is also quite possible to sponsor a website. For example, a company might contemplate sponsoring a site for a volleyball tournament, or an outdoor concert.

Here we have a list of newer interactive advertising formats:

- **YouTube videos:** Ordinary consumers often use YouTube to upload content, but marketing professionals can also use it to upload advertisements. YouTube videos are covered later in this chapter.
- **SMS promotional messages:** Here we have short text messages, either opt-in or opt-out, that one receives on a cellular telephone. Mobile marketing is covered in Chapter 18.
- **Sponsored apps:** Companies are writing mobile applications that perform useful tasks for or entertain consumers and provide promotional opportunities for those same companies.
- **Advergames:** These are hedonic pastimes that may run on game platforms, tablets, phones or the Web. Consumers have fun and the companies generate awareness and receive other benefits.
- **Email messages:** Firms sometimes offer opt-in newsletters, but of course there is also spam, which is in fact impossible to opt out of.
- **Web ads that reside on web pages:** Here we include banner advertisements, buttons, skyscrapers or podcasts. They share the property that they appear as part of a web page.
- **Web ads that emerge from web pages:** This category includes interstitials, pop-ups and pop-unders. Here the ads do not appear to be part of the content of the page; instead they end up in a separate window on the desktop, or end up in the same window but in between two pages of content. Both types of Web ads are covered in this chapter.
- **Snapchat:** Advertisers usually want their ads to stick around, but unlike other categories of advertising, snaps are designed to disappear. Firms are beginning to explore the use of this platform for exchanging photos or video. Snaps feel very authentic, and are ideal for experimenting with promotional approaches since any snap will disappear within one to ten seconds.
- **Keyword search advertising:** This approach has, of course, been developed most famously by Google, a company that allows large and small businesses to purchase search terms and bid to appear on the results page. Keyword advertising, also called search engine marketing, is covered in this chapter.

- **Corporate websites:** Here we have the basic company home page that serves as a point of presence on the World Wide Web. Such sites are maintained by almost every medium-sized and large business in the world, and numerous small firms as well. How to design these sorts of communication websites is the topic of several chapters in this book.
- **Social advertising:** More and more marketers are harnessing the target consumer's social network to help sell. If many of my friends like a certain product, this might be enough to convince me to become a customer too. The advertising potential of social media remains murky, however.

Each of the above communication vehicles has different properties, but they share one key component of all digital communication – they are accountable and therefore amenable to analytical modeling. For example, the probability of a clickthrough on a banner or search ad can be captured and experiments can be run to determine the best choice of words. The above list of vehicles does differ, however, in terms of how much control they leave in the hands of the viewer and how intrusive they tend to be on the viewer's activity. For example, spam arrives in the user's email inbox regardless of whether the user wishes to see the ad or not. On the other hand, a corporate website is entirely non-intrusive, as the viewer needs to voluntarily arrive on the site to view any promotional message. Related to intrusiveness, but not identical to it, is the distinction between inbound and outbound marketing (also briefly discussed in Chapter 1). Email, banners and SMS are examples of outbound marketing while web pages and search advertising typify inbound marketing.

Given all these options, it is difficult for companies to optimize their promotional spending. A technique known as integrated marketing communication (IMC) (Sheehan and Doherty, 2001) has been put forward to help firms coordinate their multichannel communication mix. It is often the case that the right mix of different formats will work better than spending all the money on a single format. Another way to say this is that the firm can create communication synergy if it optimizes its mix.

Web advertisements

At this point we are going to focus on ads that either emerge from web pages or reside on web pages such as the classic banner ad. Later we will discuss advertisements that appear on search result web pages – that is, keyword search advertising.

Web advertisements occur on the Internet, which is of course a network. This highlights the fact that Web ads are a phenomenon that requires we

Figure 14.1 The
nature and quality
of the connection
between a banner ad
and its payoff page
will depend on the
hosting page for the
advertisement

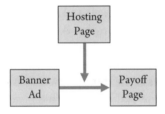

connect three networked pieces: the hosting page, the banner itself and the payoff page. (A potential fourth box that might be labeled "Purchase" could be positioned on the left on Figure 14.1). In Figure 14.1, the relationship between the ad and the payoff page is moderated by the hosting page. In other words, the effectiveness with which the ad will send visitors to the payoff page depends on which hosting page you pick. We therefore begin with that topic.

The hosting page

To compare television and the Internet, we might ask ourselves the question, "How many channels does the Internet have?" One firm estimates that the number of different websites was 1.8 billion as of its January 2017 survey (Netcraft, 2017).

Even if you have digital cable, the chances are that this is a bigger number than the number of channels you get at home on TV! Picking a hosting page is obviously not going to be like picking a TV channel for advertising.

We can describe the popularity of a network node using the Power Law, illustrated in Figure 14.2. The Power Law suggests that the probability of a page having n visitors is proportional to $n^{-\gamma}$,

$$\Pr(n) \propto n^{-\gamma},$$

where the ∞ symbol means "is proportional to" and $\Pr(n)$ is the probability that a page has n visitors. On the Web, γ has been estimated as being around 2, although Figure 14.2 is for illustrative purposes only and uses a value of 1. In general, this formula means that there are far more small sites than large sites. These small sites are ideal for the purposes of advertising since they allow for targeted, customized communication. Perhaps the one problem is finding them, but advertising networks, as well as Google, among other companies, helps to automatically match advertisers with small sites using its AdSense program. Television ads, on the other hand, follow more of a shot-

Figure 14.2 The frequency distribution for page popularity follows a Power Law. Note both axes are drawn on a log scale – we are counting zeroes

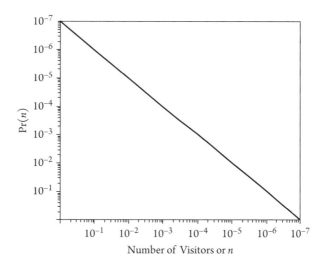

gun approach, with advertisers trying to find the largest possible audience that more or less matches the demographics of the target market.

There are inevitable tradeoffs when we contemplate the hosting page. In general, the more targeted the audience, exposing your ad to that audience will cost more per contact. And speaking of costs, there are three different ways that the owner of the hosting page might charge:

- **CPM pricing:** This acronym stands for cost per 1000 where M is the Roman numeral for 1000. Under this pricing scheme, the advertising firm pays a fixed amount for every time an audience member is exposed to the ad. For example, if the audience consists of 2000 people and you have charged me $40 for the privilege of exposing my ad once to each of them, then my CPM is $20.
- **Clickthrough pricing:** You only pay if someone clicks on your advertisement. As we shall see, Google uses this method of selling ad space. Recently, there has been a problem with what is known as click fraud. Certain hosting page owners have been known to click on ads themselves to increase their revenue. Competitors have also been known to click on other firms' ads.
- **Outcome pricing:** Here you pay only if there is some revenue-generating outcome on your website. For example, Amazon will pay you to place a book ad on your site, but only if someone clicks on the ad and then buys the book.

Often, page owners will give you a trial period to allow you to figure out how much benefit you will receive from your ad run. Of course, you may have to pay more to have exclusivity – that is, to be the only advertiser on a particular page or site, or at least the only advertiser from your product category. You may also find yourself paying for the better page positions, and obviously a bigger ad will be more expensive than a smaller ad. We turn to this topic next.

The ad itself

Choosing an ad is a mix between creativity and analytics. Creativity is needed to produce new ads and analytics are needed to assess the performance of the ads in terms of the goals of the company. Simply put, we can say that the advertiser wishes to create an ad that produces the highest response. One new approach to creating ads is to break them into "genes," and then use a genetic algorithm to pick the most "fit" ad, in other words, the ads that produce the highest response. Then pieces of the winning ads (colors, words, images, shape) are recombined into new ads, and the contest is repeated.

There are a number of standard advertisement sizes on the Web. We note that the size of the ad determines how much text you can write on it, so it has quite an impact on the kind of message you can convey. A bigger banner also takes up more space in the visitor's peripheral vision and is more likely to be noticed or attended to (attention is discussed in Chapter 10). The most popular sizes include:

- leader board   728 × 90;
- classic banner   468 × 60;
- skyscraper   120 × 600;
- button   120 × 90.

The above numbers represent a count of pixels, with the number of columns given first and the number of rows given second. Your ad will no doubt consist of a set of words (known as copy) and images. The words and images you choose might well reflect your communication goals as described above, including cognition, affect or behavior, and also whether you are using a central or peripheral route to persuading the folks who see the ad to click or buy.

The payoff page

One difference between a flexible network like the Internet that is built from software, and a mass medium like TV, is that when a Web user lands on your ad, you know where he or she came from. It is therefore possible to coordinate the following sequence: (1) hosting page; (2) banner ad; and (3) payoff page (see Figure 14.1 earlier). All three elements must logically match each other. The hosting page is chosen because it captures a particular microsegment, the ad is explicitly targeted to that microsegment and to the specific topic of the hosting page, and the payoff page is designed to provide follow up information on the same specific topic along with persuasive text and images for the advertised good or service. For example, if we own a site selling bicycles we might place a banner advertisement on a magazine article on Olympic cyclist Kristin Armstrong. The banner ad might also mention Kristin, and when visitors click on this ad, we definitely do not link them to our home page. Instead we should link to the model of bike that Kristin rides, along with a testimonial from the athlete about that model. We can use a unique URL for visitors who are arriving from that particular ad in order to coordinate the banner and the payoff page. In fact, we should use a different URL for every version of every banner ad. This gives us the ability to perform an active experiment (Chapter 4) and thereby figure out which banner ad is more effective by active experimentation.

Management of a banner ad campaign can be facilitated through networks of sites that join together to get a more complete view of what people are doing online. Such ad networks use either cookies or Web bugs to track a user from one site in the network to the next. Cookies (described in Chapter 3) are files written to a computer's hard drive, which may help us to know if the same computer has been used to visit different sites on the ad network. A Web bug is a one pixel transparent image (hence invisible to the user) on a web page. The site that serves this image can record the IP address as that address is observed while someone is visiting different sites in the ad network. As in all Web log data, we are actually tracking a particular computer here rather than a particular consumer. Such networks enable retargeting (Chapter 4), which occurs when a site you have previously visited throws up a banner on a different site to get you back. Retargeting is a form of what is sometimes called behavioral targeting since it is the user's behavior that leads the firm to display the ad. It should be added here that banner ad network techniques such as retargeting are considered controversial since some consumers feel they violate privacy.

Google also has a banner ad network but it uses a different model. Website owners can agree to be part of the Google AdSense network, which means that Google will serve ads on these sites that are relevant to the topic of the page. In this sense, Google ads cannot be exactly targeted to who is viewing them but they can be targeted to the page that is being viewed. In other words, the AdSense program is an example of contextual advertising, where the banner ad and the hosting page that forms the context for the ad are coordinated. Next, we investigate another example of contextual advertising – keyword search advertising. In the case of keyword advertising, the ad is coordinated with what the user is searching for at that moment.

Keyword search advertising

Google's keyword search advertising service is called AdWords. Google runs its AdWords auction in real time (online auctions are covered in Chapter 20). When someone enters keywords like "camera" or "hotel Westwood," all the companies that want to put an ad on the results page offer a bid. This bidding process takes a few fractions of a second and is, of course, executed completely by computer.

Each advertiser using the Google AdWords system sets up a maximum price that they are willing to pay. This is known as the maximum cost per click, or CPC. Advertisers can also control the dates within which they wish to bid, their daily budget, the language used by the searching consumer, and the geographical region of the search to which they wish to present the keyword ad.

If you are familiar with auctions, you might think at this point that the advertiser who makes the highest bid will win. That is not necessarily true. Google uses a concept it calls Ad Rank. Since only eight ads will appear on the results page, only the ads with the eight highest ad ranks will win (on some pages, Google restricts the results to five winners). Ad Rank is based on Google's expected revenue, which has two factors (Google, 2007) as can be seen in this equation:

$$\text{Ad rank} = \text{Bid} \times \text{Pr}(CT)$$

Bid is simply the amount bid for the placement, while $\text{Pr}(CT)$ refers to the probability of a clickthrough. The process of picking a good advertisement therefore requires more than money since the clickthrough rate figures into the formula. Since Google is paid by clickthrough pricing, Ad rank is equivalent to Google's expected or average revenue for running the ad.

Google (2007) advises that the advertiser should take the following steps to generate good keyword ads:

1. **Expand:** Start by brainstorming keywords. Just shoot keywords out of your mind. Draft a set of ads that go with different keywords.
2. **Match:** Next pick your keyword match types. You can go with a broad match where you bid on any of your keywords or an exact match where you only bid if all of your keywords are in the consumer's search. You can

also pick negative keywords, which are words that if present cancel your bid.

3. **Scrub:** Keep your best and delete the rest.
4. **Group:** Create multiple groups of ads, each driven from different keywords.
5. **Refine:** Test and change depending on your results. Since ad rank depends on both the bid amount and the predicted clickthrough, the higher your predicted clickthrough rate, the lower your cost per click (CPC). Thus, CPC is a good indicator of a quality campaign. In the tradition of direct marketing, the goal is to continuously test to find ads with ever higher clickthroughs and therefore ever lower CPCs.

YouTube

A company can use its YouTube home page like a private broadcasting network for informational or entertaining product videos. YouTube allows a commercial, shot for outbound marketing, to be used, or inbound marketing, or firms may shoot a longer version just for YouTube. Blendtec is a small manufacturer of blenders that has experienced immense success with YouTube videos. The company began filming brief two-minute presentations of their blenders pulverizing any object you can imagine, such as tin cans, hockey pucks, and an iPhone! The videos not only demonstrated the strength and power of their blenders, but also added an entertainment dimension to generate engagement, comments and sharing. Often the amazement generated from watching bizarre objects being ground up in a Blendtec blender would induce a cascade of sharing via email or social media. In such cases one would say that the videos had "gone viral." This expression refers to the rapid propagation of word-of-mouth information and is more generally known as viral marketing, discussed further in Chapter 24.

YouTube affords companies the opportunity to bypass mainstream television networks with advertisements that are too risqué or inappropriate for TV. Some firms therefore shoot multiple versions of commercials and place the more controversial version on YouTube. Here we refer to campaigns by GoDaddy.com, Axe body wash, and Bud Light among others. Any marketer using controversy to sell must realize that such a strategy can hurt long-term profitability. Needless to say, there are numerous ethical concerns with some of these practices (see Chapter 5). A safer practice, although one that is not itself without risk, is for firms to create contests in which ordinary consumers create their own ads. Such consumer-generated content is discussed in Chapter 23.

? QUESTIONS AND EXERCISES

1 How should online advertising change over the product life cycle?

2 We might categorize advertising format according to intrusiveness – do they intrude on what the viewer is doing, or are they part of what the user is doing? Another way to say this is that with some advertising formats, the user has more control (corporate website) and the advertiser has relatively less control. With other formats, the user has less control and the advertiser assumes relatively more control (spam email). Go through each format discussed in the section "Types of electronic marketing communications" and rank them with respect to how much control users have. Be prepared to justify your ranking.

3 We also might categorize advertising according to the distinction between owned media and paid media. Go through the list of newer advertising formats and categorize each format as owned or paid.

4 Assume that you make tennis rackets and are running two banner ad campaigns, one placed on a diet and exercise website, and another campaign on a site for very serious tennis players. For both ads, consider the sequence: hosting page–banner ad–payoff page. How would you customize the two ads across the three elements?

5 Imagine you are participating in the Google AdWords service on behalf of a store that sells various items such as clothing with your university's symbols and logos. Come up with keywords for driving traffic to that shop's web page. What sort of matches would you use? What negative keywords would you use?

6 Given your answer to question 5 above, now write a Google ad for the same store. Note that the usual Google ads have a maximum of 25 characters for the ad title, up to 70 characters (35 characters per line for up to two lines) for the ad text, and 35 characters for a display URL.

7 Unlike many auctions where the firm with the most money wins, the formula for Ad Rank depends on the probability of a clickthrough and not just the bid amount. We know this formula optimizes Google's clickthrough revenue. What is the impact of this change on the types of ads that advertisers develop?

8 Discuss the potential of social networking sites like Facebook or Google+ as an advertising medium. How or why would a firm wish to advertise on one of those sites? Is this an intrusive form of advertising where advertisers have more control, or rather, is it a form with more user control? Are there certain products that might be amenable to advertising on a social network site?

9 Using gaming platforms for advertising is a new format for marketers. Sometimes companies sponsor the game and sometimes the ad is placed in the game in the way that products are placed in movies. What are the advantages and disadvantages of these two approaches? What products would be best suited to the two approaches?

REFERENCES

Google, Inc. (2007), *Marketing and Advertising Using Google: Targeting Your Advertising to the Right Audience*, Cincinnati, OH: Atomic Dog Publishing, pp. 53–5.

Netcraft, Inc. (2017), "January 2017 Web Server Survey," accessed February 8, 2018 at https://news.netcraft.com/archives/2017/01/12/january-2017-web-server-survey.html.

Petty, R., J.T. Cacioppo and D. Schumann (1983), "Central and peripheral routes to advertising effectiveness: The moderating role of involvement," *Journal of Consumer Research*, **10** (2), 135–46.

Sheehan, K.B. and C. Doherty (2001), "Re-weaving the Web: Integrating print and online communications," *Journal of Interactive Marketing*, **15** (2), 47–59.

Section III

Digital networks as a distribution channel

The Internet and other related networks represent alternative retail channels. Unlike mass media, the Internet is addressable and therefore creates a direct channel to the consumer. In effect, the retailing function can be translated to software and provided to customers online.

The first part of this section comprises two chapters (15 and 16) that cover how consumers go about the tasks necessary for shopping. In addition to being enjoyable, shopping can be thought of as a series of problem-solving steps. After these two chapters, in Chapter 17, the focus turns to the specific nature of direct channels and how they are different from typical retail. In Chapter 18, we take a quick look at mobile marketing. Next, Chapter 19 outlines important aspects of strategy for online sellers. This section finishes with Chapters 20 and 21 on B2B online selling.

15

Consumer problem solving online

We now begin discussing the use of digital networks as a distribution channel. This changes our focus from one of communication and relationships, to one of retailing, selling and purchasing. In this chapter, we focus on the consumer, and we conceptualize the purchase process as a series of consumer problem-solving steps, an approach made explicit in a famous consumer behavior book by Blackwell, Miniard and Engel (2001). Such problem solving may be relatively routine (we call this, of course, routine problem solving), as might occur when consumers are not particularly involved in the product category or where the products are relatively undifferentiated with attributes that do not produce any possible risk. On the other hand, the problem solving might be non-routine but still limited, or it might be extended. Extended problem solving occurs when there are lots of brands that are hard to categorize, numerous product attributes, no time pressure, and the potential for risk.

Given a particular level of involvement in the problem-solving task, the consumer will then either zoom through the steps of decision making (low-involvement, routine problem solving) or take a careful, long look at the purchase (high-involvement, extended problem solving). Here are the steps of consumer problem solving (Blackwell, Miniard and Engel, 2001):

1. problem recognition;
2. search;
3. alternative evaluation;
4. purchase behavior; and
5. post-purchase evaluation.

We now talk about each of these in turn, with the exception of search. Search is the step from the above list that is perhaps most radically changed by digital networks, so it will have a chapter of its own – Chapter 16.

Problem recognition

This stage kicks off when the consumer becomes aware of a gap between what the consumer has and the product the consumer wants. One way to conceptualize goods and services is to think of them as a bundle of features. In fact, we use a number of words to describe product features: dimensions, attributes and characteristics. Whatever phrase we choose, these characteristics deliver benefits and consumers are frequently aware of them. Banner advertisements (Chapter 14) can help to push the awareness of different product characteristics and highlight the difference between the product in hand and the ideal product.

Evaluation

As mentioned above, we are saving the search stage for the next chapter. Now we analyze evaluation. In the economic theory of rational man, consumers are assumed to choose by carefully evaluating all the characteristics of each product, and by thinking about how important each of those characteristics might be. In this sense, each product gets a meticulously calculated overall score, much like you might receive a total score for an overall class grade. Each assignment or test is like a different product attribute, for example miles per gallon, color or price. Your score on some assignments might be better than on others, just as the brand's score on some attributes might be higher than on others. You might like the price but not the color, or vice versa. In addition to the score for each attribute, each attribute also has a weight (the aptly named attribute weight). Just as a final exam might be worth more than a quiz, for some consumers the price might be more important than the color. Rational man combines each of the product attributes, weighs them in terms of importance, and reaches an overall conclusion about the attractiveness of the brand. We can summarize this with an equation for the attractiveness of brand $i - (A_i)$ – in other words, the consumer's evaluation of brand i:

$$A_i = \sum_j w_j \cdot b_{ij}$$

In the above equation, w_j is the attribute weight for the jth attribute, specifying how important that attribute is – that is, how much weight it has. The more important product attribute j is, the bigger the value of w_j. The symbol b_{ij} represents the belief in the extent to which product i contains attribute j. When information from all the product attributes is taken into account by the consumer, as in the above equation, so that a good score on one attribute can overcome a bad score on a different attribute, we say that the consumer is following a compensatory evaluation rule. It is critical for marketers to know which product attributes are important to the consumer. In other words, it is critical to know the values of the w_j.

In the psychological theory of the cognitive miser, consumers are assumed to want to come to a reasonable conclusion as easily as possible. Rather than combining all the information – how well each brand scored on each attribute and how important those attributes are – cognitive misers look for shortcuts or heuristics to make quicker and easier decisions. Many heuristics involve the elimination or disqualification of certain brands. For example, you might start with the most important attribute (for you, maybe mileage) and compare the brands on that. The car with the best mileage wins, without considering any other attribute. If there is a tie, you might have to go down to the second most important attribute, but you can see that this heuristic, called a lexicographic evaluation rule, is a real time saver! Another heuristic is simply to pick the most popular brand, a gambit known as the popularity heuristic. How bad could the most popular choice be?

We can help consumers evaluate the brands by personalizing, in various ways, the display of product information. We can help them by reminding them of their previous choices. We can allow them to sort the brands by any attribute: price, service quality, pixels, color, size, ratings, popularity and so on. Our site can also provide organizational structure for the consumer by grouping the brands, organizing them into classification schemes or otherwise emphasizing patterns among the competing choice options. If we think that consumers might want to use an elimination heuristic, we can help them by filtering the choice set and thereby eliminate some brands for them.

Brands and their attributes represent a common example of a faceted information space, as presented in Chapter 13. In terms of navigating such a space, we can give the consumer the ability to process brand by brand, clicking from one brand to the next, or we can allow the consumer to process attribute by attribute, moving from price to color and color to material. If they are navigating from brand to brand, we can show them all the attributes for each brand, or just those attributes that are more heavily weighted. If they are navigating from attribute to attribute, we can show them all the brands or just the best brands on that attribute. If we think that consumers might use the popularity heuristic we can sort by popularity.

All those choices must be made by the online retailer, who has full control over navigation design and the information mix presented to consumers. In general, a relationship-friendly strategy will be that strategy that helps the consumer make better decisions, even if those decisions do not optimize the current transaction. The goal is to generate repeat business, grow customer equity and add to our knowledge about the consumer (see Chapter 7). The transaction of the moment is of secondary importance.

Purchase behavior

E-tail sites are heavily afflicted by shopping cart abandonment. This problem makes it clear that we have to make it as easy as possible for the consumer to actually "pull the trigger" and execute the transaction. In addition to making purchase easy, a wish list can allow consumers to save their choices even though they did not buy on this site visit.

Post-purchase evaluation

This final step of consumer problem solving is very important simply because customer retention is very important! What we need to worry about here is a different gap – this time, a gap between the consumer's expectations and the actual performance of our site (also discussed in Chapter 2). This gap might form due to any of the following:

- **Time required to order:** Poor site design can create a gap here if it is too difficult to buy or the site information space is poorly conveyed to the would-be buyer.
- **Time to ship:** Here the key factor is the amount of inventory liquidity – that is, how much of a particular product is on hand to ship out.
- **Time to delivery:** Here our performance depends on the variety and quality of shipping options we offer, and how many warehouses we have and their locations.
- **Returns processing:** Getting shipped items back to the warehouse is called reverse logistics.

The above list forms the part of purchase known as fulfillment. In other words, fulfillment consists of actually executing and finalizing the transaction, up to and including delivery.

The gap between fulfillment expectations and fulfillment performance can be closed in two ways. First, you can carefully manage expectations by being upfront and honest about what sort of performance the consumer should expect. Second, you can manage performance by spending more money on fulfillment operations.

After the purchase, the website can provide a variety of supplementary services such as allowing for order confirmation and shipping updates. There are also many ways to add value to the purchase, after the purchase. The site might include guides, manuals, tips, repair tracking, FAQs, warranty exposition, technical support, opt-in email services and a personalized profile, or offer a virtual community. In particular, hosting a virtual community can create a good deal of added value and so this topic gets a chapter of its own – Chapter 24.

 QUESTIONS AND EXERCISES

1   This assignment uses Table 15.1 presented below. Assume you are working for a retailing website that sells brands A, B, C and D in a particularly profitable product category. Your job in this assignment is to calculate which brand the consumer would choose if the customer were to use (a) the lexicographic rule; and (b) the compensatory rule. Finally, (c) assume that brand D has the highest margin for the e-tailer and that the e-tailer therefore wants to somehow push brand D. How should it go about doing so? How could we arrange the display of the brands or the website such that the consumer would be more likely to choose brand D? Specifically, use the results of parts (a) and (b) to formulate your answer.

Table 15.1 A hypothetical table containing brand beliefs, cut-offs, and attribute weights for four attributes

Attribute	Attribute Weights	Brand Beliefs			
		A	B	C	D
Taste	1	5	5	4	5
Price	2	4	3	5	2
Nutrition	3	3	3	1	5
Convenience	4	2	3	3	5
Cut-offs		3	3	3	3

2   How would an e-tail website help support consumers under conditions of routine problem solving? How about when the consumer engages in limited problem solving? How about when the consumer is engaging in extended problem solving?

3   How does it help a marketer to know the w_j importance weight values discussed in this chapter? What can we do with this information?

4   For the following types of offerings, note whether you think consumers might use compensatory evaluation, lexicographic evaluation, the popularity heuristic, or some other evaluation method:
    (a)   news articles presented on a news website;
    (b)   music purchases;

(c)   shoes;

(d)   external computer hard drive.

 REFERENCE

Blackwell, R.D., P.W. Miniard and J.F. Engel (2001), *Consumer Behavior*, ninth edition, Chicago, IL: The Dryden Press.

16

Consumer search

As you should remember from the previous chapter, here are the steps of consumer problem solving:

1. problem recognition – awareness of a gap between what I have and what I want;
2. search – the topic of this chapter;
3. alternative evaluation – working out the preferred option to buy;
4. purchase behavior – performing the steps necessary to execute the transaction; and
5. post-purchase evaluation – comparing purchase expectations with purchase performance.

A consumer behavior textbook written by Blackwell, Miniard and Engel (2001) popularized this way of thinking about consumer behavior. We now delve deeply into search – the step from the above list that is perhaps changed the most by the Internet. Chapter 14 covers keyword search advertising.

Searching on the Internet

Traditionally, we have thought of consumers as searching in stores, by reading, or by talking with friends – a process known as word-of-mouth (discussed in Chapter 24). Word-of-mouth is also covered in Chapter 25, but for now we focus on three "levels" of online search: searching across the Internet, searching within a site, and searching on a particular page.

First, consumers search across the Internet to find appropriate websites. At this level, we use careful Hypertext Markup Language (HTML) coding to make sure that our site can be found. The title markup is important here, and is illustrated below:

```
<title the-page-title-goes-here>
```

The title appears in the "Title bar" on the Web browser, and also serves to create a caption for Web bookmarks or favorites. Search engines also weigh the information in the title markup, assuming that Web authors typically summarize their web pages using that markup. There is also a technique called meta-tagging in which we pick keywords (word1, word2, . . .) to describe our site:

```
<meta http-equiv="Keywords" content="word1, word2, •••">
```

Search engines also use HTML keywords, at least somewhat, to help decide if a site is relevant to a user keyword search. Unfortunately, both the title and meta tag techniques can be gamed, meaning that unscrupulous webmasters attempt to trick Google into giving their pages a high ranking. The end result has been that Google and other search engines do not rely greatly on those techniques. Instead, Google calculates a quantity known as the PageRank. PageRank is a recursive function of incoming links to the site. If a page that links to our page has a high PageRank, this gives *our* page a high PageRank. The more high-quality incoming links we have, the higher our PageRank. In some sense, our site's PageRank is a little like word-of-mouth since it is given to us as an expression of worthiness by other sites. Lately, some site owners have tried to game PageRank by joining link farms. A link farm is a set of sites that agree to link to the other sites in the set just to increase their search engine ranking. This technique is not very effective. The main secret to raising the Google PageRank of the pages on our site is to make them worthy of being linked to by others.

In addition to the basic principle of making your page linkworthy, you can easily make your site more search engine friendly by adding explanatory text to a variety of HTML markups. For example, when you have an image on the page, make sure you fill out the "alt" text field. Link anchor text (between the <a> and the </a>) should be meaningful and related to the way you want the target page to be indexed. You should make sure the topic of the page, its keywords as it were, are mentioned at least once, but possibly more than once, in the body of the page.

Of course, we can also use banner advertisements or keyword purchases to help drive traffic to our site. These techniques are discussed in Chapter 14. Finally, our domain name should be something that consumers might naturally try to type in, and be memorable as well.

At the second level, consumers search within websites to find pages or products of interest. We spent time in Chapter 13 talking about the notion of navigability of websites. In effect, you want consumers to easily understand where they have been on your site, where they are now, and how to get to where they want to go. To the extent to which the consumer can glean a mental model of your information space, that consumer can easily search your site. Your within-site search function should also work well. Third, assuming voluntary attention, consumers visually search within web pages to find the exact information they seek. The notions of page design covered in Chapters 10 and 11 are quite relevant here.

How much do consumers search?

There are benefits and costs to search. The main benefit of search is to reduce the uncertainty surrounding a purchase. To put this in a slightly different way, it is usually the case that the seller has more information about the offering than the buyer. We often refer to this as information asymmetry. The consumer engages in search to level the playing field somewhat, reducing the information asymmetry.

The costs to searching might not be so obvious, but recall the psychological theory of the cognitive miser (Chapter 15). In addition to the cost of thinking, there is the opportunity cost of the time and money spent searching. The very act of searching delays the decision as well as the benefits of the purchase. Online there is some physical effort involved when the buyer moves the mouse, types or scrolls. There is also mental effort involved in online search, since the consumer must pay attention, and read and comprehend what is appearing on the screen. Taking all these into account, we can say that, even online, search costs are real.

In general, the problem with offline search is the difficulty of finding options worth pursuing. Oddly enough, the problem with online search is the ease of finding options worth pursuing. Online, search costs are generated as the consumer tries to work through what might be termed an "embarrassment of riches." This suggests the importance of stopping rules in online consumer search behavior. When do you say "That's enough, I have seen plenty of options, I know what I am going to buy"? When you quit depends on what is at stake, and search is much reduced under conditions of routine problem solving. Conversely, extended problem solving extends the amount of search. Search also depends on the distribution of product characteristics. For example, if all the products seem to be the same, why keep searching? On the other hand, if there is significant variability or dispersion of product attributes – price comes to mind as an obvious example – the consumer will need to search more to reduce the information asymmetry present in the market.

In a perfect world, we would have as much time as we needed to make sure we always bought the ideal offering. Instead, we are likely to satisfice rather than satisfy ourselves. Satisficing is an example of a heuristic (heuristics are discussed in Chapter 15). Satisficing is a method for choosing among serially presented alternatives in which the consumer sets an aspiration level and stops as soon as some alternative meets or exceeds that level. Of course, satisficing does not guarantee you will end up with the exact perfect purchase.

In general, consumer search depends on a variety of factors, including perceived time pressure, personal involvement and relevance, the consumer's optimum stimulation level, various skill factors and comfort with technology, the consumer's search and information processing skills, and how much knowledge the consumer has. Oddly enough, amount of knowledge produces a non-linear result. Moderate category knowledge leads to more search. Experts' search is more efficient so they do not need to search as long. Novices, on the other hand, don't even know they need to search! Thus, people with moderate category knowledge search the most. The more product-specific information you already know, the less you need to search, but the more general product-class information you have, the more you search. Punj and Staelin (1983) have investigated the topic of how knowledge impacts search.

Product characteristics and search

The nature of the product category also impacts search. Purchase conspicuousness, the presence of linked purchase decisions, the length of commitment, the number of brands in the product category, the product value-expressiveness, safety factors, and the presence of information asymmetry all have an effect on the amount of search performed.

Speaking of information asymmetry, it is traditional to categorize products or product features based on how much information asymmetry exists with respect to those products or features:

- **Search characteristics:** These are characteristics, features or attributes of the offering that can be discovered during the search process.
- **Experience characteristics:** Such characteristics can only be discovered after purchase. Examples typically include either difficult technical factors, or purely subjective factors. The attributes of services, which must be experienced to be consumed, are always experience characteristics. When experience characteristics exist, marketers sometimes try to signal the quality in advance using guarantees and return policies, or by allowing the quality to be sampled in some way.

- **Credence characteristics:** These can never be known by the consumer for certain. They are either taken on faith or not believed.

Product category and search

Source: Murphy and Enis (1986).

Figure 16.1 Four product categories based on risk and costs

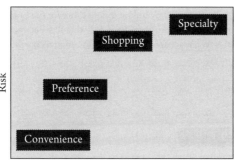

Another way to categorize products is to think in terms of costs and risk. Costs include both monetary costs and search costs (Figure 16.1). Murphy and Enis (1986) conceive of four types of goods:

- **Convenience goods** are commodities, emergency or impulse items such as batteries, staples, gum, bananas or taxi cabs. Convenience goods have low costs and low risk.
- **Preference goods** include package goods like beer, soft drinks, toothpaste, work gloves and TV channels. These goods have more costs and risks than convenience goods.
- **Shopping goods** are classic consumer durables such as autos, clothing, furniture, dentists or apartment rental. Here costs (total effort) are even higher, as is risk.
- **Specialty goods** involve the highest amount of costs or effort and risks. In this category we see "non-substitutable" brands like Ikea, Apple, Lotus sports cars and particular criminal attorneys.

Finally, following Lal and Sarvary (1999), we might modify the above lists and think about dividing all products and product characteristics into digital characteristics and non-digital characteristics.

? **QUESTIONS AND EXERCISES**

1 What is the role of branding in the search process? Be prepared to discuss this in terms of the e-tailer and e-tail branding but also in terms of a product sold by an e-tailer and that product's branding.
2 Describe the potential role of virtual communities and social media in the purchase process when there are experience characteristics.

3 According to Janiszewski (1998), we should distinguish between goal-directed search, such as might occur with functional products or where a pressing current need exists, and exploratory search, which is more likely with expressive products, and when the consumer is not explicitly looking to buy at this moment. How might online search processes function in these two different cases?

4 Consider the Murphy and Enis (1986) list of products: convenience, preference, shopping and specialty. Discuss how selling online should differ for the four product types.

5 Lal and Sarvary (1999) propose that we distinguish between digital and non-digital product characteristics. What are some digital and non-digital characteristics for:
   (a) automobiles;
   (b) wine;
   (c) clothing;
   (d) books.

 REFERENCES

Blackwell, R.D., P.W. Miniard and J.F. Engel (2001), *Consumer Behavior*, ninth edition, Chicago, IL: The Dryden Press.

Janiszewski, C. (1998), "The influence of display characteristics on visual exploratory search behavior," *Journal of Consumer Research*, **25** (3), 290–301.

Lal, R. and M. Sarvary (1999), "When and how is the Internet likely to decrease price competition?" *Marketing Science*, **18** (4), 485–503.

Murphy, P.E. and B.M. Enis (1986), "Classifying products strategically," *Journal of Marketing*, **50** (3), 24–42.

Punj, G.N. and R. Staelin (1983), "A model of consumer information search behavior for new automobiles," *Journal of Consumer Research*, **9** (4), 366–80.

17

Channels and direct channels

This chapter begins by reviewing the notion of channels. What is a channel? Why are there channels? Next, the chapter will focus on direct channels and what we already know about direct channel customers. We finish up by talking about multichannel marketing and distribution.

Channel analysis raises a number of fundamental questions. Marketers must carefully plan and execute channel strategy and choice of channels must be coordinated with care. Power and negotiation in distribution channels can be very important. For example, if Ford began selling cars online direct to the consumer, what would Ford dealerships think of this? Surely this would create channel conflict and not be productive? Before we dive deeper into thinking about channels, we might ask, what exactly do we mean by channels and by channel strategy?

Distribution channels

> A channel is structure of independent organizations within which goods, ownership, communication, payment, and risk move from, and to, the consumer.
> (Kotler, 2003)

Why are there channels at all? Why don't firms reach vertically all the way to the customer? To put this another way, what do channel members do to deserve their place in the distribution chain? The answer to these questions arises from the fact that channel members may specialize and compete in a specific role such as customer contact, promotion, negotiation, market research, market knowledge, or finance. Channel members also handle discrepancies of quantity or assortment, break bulk (reduce the purchased quantity into amounts that are closer to that which is consumed at one time), sort, and assort. A discrepancy of quantity occurs whenever production or supply quantities do not match consumption or demand quantities. For example, a printing press produces millions of copies of a book, but each consumer only wants to buy and read one. A discrepancy of assortment might occur when a certain farmer produces corn, another farmer produces lima beans, but the consumer wants to eat succotash, a dish consisting of both. Likewise, channel members may accumulate or store products to handle discrepancies of time, as might occur when a chocolate factory produces chocolate eggs year-round, but the demand for that product spikes towards the Easter holiday. In general, channel members perform physical distribution and take risks that firms further away from the customer are not willing to take. From this background, we might assume that Amazon has certain capabilities that book publishers cannot easily reproduce, or that US retailer Best Buy's website management has certain advantages over LG's such that Best Buy is more capable of selling TVs to customers than LG.

It will be useful to cover some additional channel terminology. Wholesalers and retailers are channel firms that take title, or ownership, to the goods being distributed via the channel. Conversely, a broker is an independent entity who facilitates transactions but does not take title. An agent is any firm or individual that represents the buyer or seller in a channel negotiation.

Direct selling

Direct selling via catalogs and 800/0800 numbers has been going on for some time. We know from longstanding research on these channels that direct marketing customers are more confident, adventurous, innovative, price-conscious, and cosmopolitan and tend to have higher socioeconomic status than customers who do not engage in direct marketing purchases.

The focus on this chapter is not primarily catalogs or 800/0800 numbers, but e-tail. In this and other chapters when we use the expression "e-tail" or "e-tailer," we must admit that there are a variety of different online retail activity types. We have the virtual merchant model, followed by such firms as Amazon who do not have any offline branches. We have the manufacturer-direct model as represented by firms such as Dell who also tend to sell directly, but who make what they sell. There are multichannel merchants – call them bricks & clicks – exemplified by retailers such as Barnes & Noble and Blackwell's, and catalog merchants like L.L. Bean and Grattan who follow a paper & clicks model. Finally, some firms do not sell any offline products like books, clothing or computers at all. These firms offer electronic goods and services and follow an Internet pure play model. Pure play firms will be covered in the chapters in Section IV.

Of course, every channel has its advantages and disadvantages. In the next part of this chapter we talk about the disadvantages of the Internet channel to the shopper. Next, we will discuss the advantages of the Internet to the shopper, then we will look at what advantages the Internet offers the e-tail marketer. Since the mobile channel is new and interesting in its own right, it will be covered in its own chapter – Chapter 18.

Why would a consumer not shop online?

Here is a partial list of disadvantages and costs to online shopping:

- **No computer:** Not everyone has a computer at home.
- **Low screen resolution:** While impressive in some respects, a computer screen has relatively low resolution compared to a paper catalog and is nowhere near the resolution capacity of the human eye. Screen resolution is discussed in Chapter 12.
- **Deferred consumption:** The buyer must wait for shipping.
- **No trying on and no touch:** In Chapter 16, a distinction is made between digital and non-digital characteristics. Some consumers might not want to buy an item without being able to touch it first. But tactile information about a product changes from being a search characteristic to being an experience characteristic as we move from an offline to an online channel.
- **Shipping problems:** Arranging delivery can be difficult, inconvenient and more expensive than tossing it in the trunk of your car. Returns can be even more difficult.
- **Insufficient trust:** Many consumers are still reluctant to buy online. The lack of tangibility in the online channel makes customers wary.
- **Privacy issues:** Data have been lost to hackers and sold to the highest bidder in the past. The mass media are always filled with stories about identity theft, credit card theft, and frightening scenarios are easy to conjure up.
- **Site complexity:** Site designers often create opaque and difficult online stores, making it hard for shoppers to find what they are looking for.
- **Lack of skill:** Customers vary in their technological readiness (Parasuraman, 2000). Some absolutely love interacting with and through technology while for others it is relatively painful.
- **Lack of human contact:** Many individuals crave face-to-face interaction with their fellow human beings (Curran and Meuter, 2005).

Why would a consumer shop online?

- **Selection:** Online, there are numerous niche sellers with the sort of variety that a bricks and mortar retailer could not afford. In Chapter 19, we discuss the notion of the long tail strategy and how it leverages the cost and flexibility advantages of the online channel.

- **Privacy:** One can purchase without being seen.
- **Ease of search:** The search effort involved in the online channel is, objectively speaking, less than the effort necessary for searching offline channels.
- **Ease of comparison:** Low search costs imply that comparison is relatively easy.
- **Low switching costs:** The competition is, as they say, just a mouse click away. There are also shopbots and software agents available to find the cheapest outlet.
- **Collaborative filtering:** Amazon and other e-tailers leverage customer data to help other customers search and evaluate.
- **Package delivery industry:** While shipping problems do happen, in North America and other locations, the ability to order, receive and return packages is both efficient and reliable.
- **Time advantages:** It is generally faster to get on the computer than to get in your car and drive to the mall.
- **Available 24/7:** You can access your electronic device at any time and increasingly, from anywhere, go shopping.
- **No sales pressure:** For some, not interacting with salespeople is a plus (Curran and Meuter, 2005).
- **Congestion and traffic:** The number of cars on the road has been steadily increasing for decades. This dampens enthusiasm for driving to shop and makes the online channel look better and more time efficient to the consumer.
- **Flexibility:** The digital channel can be tailored to your retail needs through customization and other examples of flexibility typified by software-based channels.
- **Information availability:** The digital channel has the capacity to be information rich.

Channel flexibility and customization

The last points about the advantages of electronic shopping highlight important strategic advantages to the merchant with respect to the Internet. Viswanathan (2005) has discussed some of these advantages. The basic flexibility of a retail channel that is built with software, as compared to one built with bricks, offers e-tailers many opportunities for optimizing the information mix – the specific information displayed to specific consumers at a specific time. Information design, at the three levels of overall site design, page design and link design, is only limited by the imagination of the e-tailer and the culturally learned assumptions of the consumer (Hofacker, 2008). As compared to a physical store, the e-tailer has control over exactly how the product appears to the consumer. In a physical store, the product itself must appear on the shelves. In a virtual store, the product is represented through images, text or other digital means. The entire online environment is under the control of the e-tailer, not the manufacturer.

There are also certain advantages that the digital channel offers in terms of customer retention. Technology sometimes exhibits the phenomenon known as lock-in. Once a consumer learns a particular interface or a particular style of interaction, switching costs can come into play, making retention easier. Switching costs are not necessarily monetary. They might involve the time or effort necessary to switch. When it gets too difficult or costly for the consumer to switch, we say that the consumer is locked in. We discuss the Law of Practice and its role in lock-in in Chapter 10.

A second advantage of the digital channel in terms of retention revolves around the notion of externalities. A positive externality is a benefit earned by one consumer without having to pay for it. Often these benefits derive from the presence of other consumers. For example, no matter what I pay for a service that lets me interact with others, if there are a lot of other people the service gives me more benefit than if there is only a small group available I can interact with. Electronic networks tend to create positive externalities generated by the presence or availability of other users. My phone becomes more valuable the more people that are available to call on it. We can see the same kind of effect leveraged by Amazon, who use data from one consumer to help other consumers make better choices. "People who bought this book also bought book X." Thus, the more consumers who buy a book from Amazon, the more Amazon can generate advice to other consumers and this establishes a competitive advantage for the firm. This competitive advantage in turn helps Amazon grow even more. We discuss externalities in detail in Chapter 23.

Multichannel marketing

A previous section of this chapter described some advantages of the digital channel. In this section, we discuss multichannel distribution. In fact, we frequently observe firms operating within multiple channels, utilizing some combination of bricks, paper or clicks. Multichannel analysis (nicely explained by Viswanathan, 2005) tells us that each channel has strengths and weaknesses, but if we create an integrated strategy across multiple channels we can create synergies between the channels. The customer will find it

Source: Verhoef, Neslin and
Vroomen (2007).

Figure 17.1 The
percentage of
consumers who gather
information on one
channel and then buy
on another channel

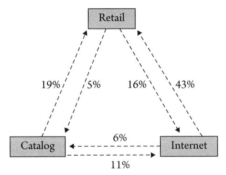

Percentage of Research Shoppers

especially convenient if all our channels are perfectly integrated to the extent
that they appear to be seamlessly connected. In that case we can say that we
have implemented an omnichannel strategy.

It can be quite difficult to achieve a seamless omnichannel. Channel conflict
may be an undesirable side-effect of multichannel marketing. Let's take as an
example a national retailer and think of ways such a firm might avoid channel
conflict and yet still offer a direct channel. One approach might be to redirect
customers to the local retail site. Another strategy might be to cut the local
retailer in, even if they did not participate in the sale.

Shoppers often search on one channel and buy on another. The percentage of
shoppers who gather information first on one channel and then use another
channel for purchase is shown in Figure 17.1 (taken from Verhoef, Neslin
and Vroomen, 2007). If the consumer spends time in the store, researching
purchase options but then buying online, the store manager does not get
credit for the sale and the consumer has not paid for the salesperson's time.
The consumer and the website that was eventually used can be said to be
free-riding off the store's labor and overhead, also called showrooming.

Another issue arising in multichannel retailing is the attribution problem.
The basic idea involves the following question: if I get a sale from a customer
who first noticed my product in a catalog, then dropped in at a store to
look at the product further, but then bought the product online (see Figure
17.1), which channel should get credit for the sale? The problem arises in
two different contexts. The manager of each of those three channels might
get a bonus based on how many sales their channel generates. So, the channel
to which I attribute the sale is pretty important to their paychecks! A second
context centers around the idea of marketing investment. In which channel
should I allocate additional funds? I want to put additional money into the

channel that gives me the highest return on investment (ROI), but it could be the case that putting a dollar into channel A creates more total sales (in channels A and B combined) than a dollar allocated to channel B. This discussion takes us to the idea of synergy, which is usually considered as a good thing. We might say we have created synergy if channel A helps channel B do a better job at creating sales, but we have to remember in that case that both channel A and channel B should be allocated funds even though the sale was physically executed by the customer in channel B.

It is worth working out all these difficulties in multichannel marketing because it is known that multichannel shoppers have a higher annual purchase volume than single channel shoppers and they are more profitable (Venkatesen, Kumar and Ravishankar, 2007).

Service quality and the cost of that service necessarily trade off, but by allowing each channel to do what it does best and what it does most efficiently, you can make the tradeoff less painful. For example, for routine questions and non-loyal customers, we might try to direct folks to the Web. On the other hand, if we have a very loyal or profitable customer with a difficult problem, we might wish to engage the customer via a face-to-face channel.

We can generate synergies using multiple channels in a variety of ways:

- create a retail location search function on your website or app;
- allow online appointment setting for in-person shopping;
- electronic bridal gift registry;
- upload an infotainment video to YouTube;
- gift certificate purchase online or offline;
- gift certificate redemption online or offline;
- allow online users to order or control paper catalog mailouts;
- in-store kiosks that allow shoppers to search your website;
- sampling and coupon distribution online, mobile or offline;
- create a version of the catalog for opt-in email; and
- use the online channel to involve customers with service co-production.

It should not be said that creating synergies is easy, however. There are incompatibilities between offline and online retailing. Online we directly ship lots of small packages to different customers, while offline the shipments from the warehouse to the retail are palletized and bigger. Online we see higher variable costs because it may be expensive to get the product the last mile (or kilometer) to the house. A retail store, on the other hand, has higher fixed costs shared among different items sold in the same location.

So, do we price the same offline and online, presenting the same image to our customers across channels? This means that we have to accept that one channel might be less profitable than it might be were it to be run by itself. But if we allow prices to vary from one channel to another, we see challenges related to free-riding and channel power discussed previously in this chapter.

QUESTIONS AND EXERCISES

1 Write up the advantages and disadvantages of the following channels:
    (a) physical retail;
    (b) paper catalog;
    (c) mobile phone.
2 I am going to take all the goods that are sold today, record the price of these goods to the consumer and also the weight of each of these. I will then create a ratio: the price per kilogram. Does this ratio allow me to predict how effective it will be to sell these goods online? Does the ratio work for both the business-to-consumer (B2C) and business-to-business (B2B) cases?
3 As mentioned in this chapter, we might assume that Amazon has certain capabilities that book publishers cannot easily reproduce, or that Best Buy's retail website has certain advantages over Sony's or LG's. What might those capabilities and advantages be? Dell, on the other hand, sells a tremendous number of computers directly to the customer. How does Dell do this while other firms cannot or do not?
4 How can the national headquarters for a series of branch locations sell online without angering the managers of those locations? Is there a way to work around the problem and to avoid free-riding problems?

REFERENCES

Curran, J.M. and M.L. Meuter (2005), "Self-service technology adoption: Comparing three technologies," *Journal of Services Marketing*, **19** (2), 103–13.

Hofacker, C.F. (2008), "E-tail constraints and tradeoffs," *Direct Marketing: An International Journal*, **2** (3), 129–43.

Kotler, P. (2003), *Marketing Management*, 11th edition, Upper Saddle River, NJ: Prentice Hall.

Parasuraman, A. (2000), "Technology Readiness Index (TRI): A multiple-item scale to measure readiness to embrace new technologies," *Journal of Service Research*, **2** (4), 307–20.

Venkatesen, R., V. Kumar and N. Ravishankar (2007), "Multichannel shopping: Causes and consequences," *Journal of Marketing*, **71** (2), 114–32.

Verhoef, P.C., S.A. Neslin and B. Vroomen (2007), "Multichannel customer management: Understanding the research-shopper phenomenon," *International Journal of Research in Marketing*, **24** (2), 129–48.

Viswanathan, S. (2005), "Competing across technology-differentiated channels: The impact of network externalities and switching costs," *Management Science*, **51** (3), 483–96.

18
Mobile devices

The world of telephony has changed greatly in the past several years, perhaps more so than any other computing domain. It is fitting that we give Apple credit for many of the changes in telephony. The company has redefined the cell phone, or perhaps putting this a different way, has created a new category of cell phone – namely, the smartphone. At the moment, Apple is in a battle with Google, whose Android cell phone operating system has been very successful and has established a competing ecology to Apple's. All over the world, cell phone networks have converted to the Internet Protocol (IP) as the basis for service provision. Likewise, cell phones have become true computers.

While your phone is a computer with a two-way radio, it no doubt has a much smaller screen and key pad, real or virtual, as compared to even a small netbook computer. This smallness changes the nature of the channel, especially compared to desktop or living room devices. For one thing, mobile services are frequently push services with social media updates, stock quotes, sports scores or weather updates being delivered to the user in the form of mobile notifications. The difficulty of using such a small device makes mobile less wide open than the Web, and therefore competition for screen space is even fiercer. On mobile phones, users prefer to access content and entertainment on dedicated apps, rather than a browser. This produces even more competition.

Mobile devices are highly useful in executing point-of-sale transactions – for example, paying your restaurant bill using your phone. Where mobile really shines is in location-based services such as searching for the right restaurant near your current location, telling you when the next bus will arrive, whether your flight is late, or in delivering a coupon for a business near where you are walking.

There are a variety of categories of mobile devices operating according to a variety of different standards.

Devices and technologies

Cellular telephones

At the time I am writing this, there are more than 7 billion mobile phones in use in the world (Wikipedia, 2018). Cell phone technology is converging on a single world standard, known as Global System for Mobile Communications (GSM). In the United States, Verizon Wireless and Sprint have committed to the latest generation of that standard, called Long-Term Evolution (LTE), leaving only a handful of small companies using a non-GSM network in the US.

In the rest of the world, consumers often switch carriers by simply pulling a SIM (Subscriber Identity Module) card out of their phones and replacing it with another one. Most users in Asia, Africa and Europe pre-pay and are not locked into long-term contracts. The per capita cell phone use in the US, the types of use, and attitudes toward the device, have in the past lagged behind Europe and Asia by several years. However, each time there is a shift in generation of cell phone technology, the cards may be shuffled once again. The long-term contracts more common in the US can lead to lower costs per minute, however.

Regardless, it is clear that the amount and type of mobile use varies greatly from area to area (Wikipedia, 2018). Usage is generally low in North America, and high in Latin America, Eastern Europe, in the Mediterranean and the Middle East, and in the Asian city states. In those places, mobile technology has affected the way people relate to each other in the sense that social planning and organizing tends to occur more in real time on an ad hoc basis rather than planned beforehand. In the US, the cell phone is still somewhat of a utilitarian product, with the benefit of being connected to work, or of safety as happens when parents give a phone to a child. Of course, the "benefit" of always being connected to work sometimes inspires more dread than satisfaction. In Europe, on the other hand, the cell phone is primarily a hedonic product. As Michael Mace (2006) describes it in his blog: "many people in Europe feel about their mobiles the way that Californians feel about their cars."

We will talk some more on the benefits of cell phone use later. First, let's look at an overview of mobile technology.

Tablets

This chapter began by crediting Apple for reinventing the smartphone. Now we must credit Apple for reinventing the tablet in the form of the iPad and its successors. Unlike phones or PDAs (personal digital assistants), tablets are generally used with both hands. Tablets can use either a cell phone signal or Wi-Fi. They seem ideally suited for quick access to email, to social media, and to browsing the Web. They are also being increasingly used in B2B contexts, as a way of accessing company data away from the desk. For example, a nurse may carry a tablet as he or she visits patients. The tablet allows him or her to easily look up a patient's history or medication schedule.

E-readers

These are tablet-like devices that are optimized for reading. Many of these devices can also access the Web, and allow for sharing via social media.

In addition to the above categories of devices, the following technologies are important in mobile:

- **Bluetooth:** This is a communications protocol that links phones, PDAs, computers, cash registers, printers, speakers and other peripherals. It is fast and only works when two devices are in proximity.
- **Wi-Fi:** This is a computer network standard that is becoming more widely available in phone-like devices. We are likely to see a blurring between Wi-Fi and cell phone network access to voice and Internet services. Wi-Fi is much faster than cell phone standards, but it doesn't handle movement of the device from one base station to another very well.
- **Near-field communication:** These are standards for allowing phone-to-phone communication in very near proximity. Ironically, the inconvenience of having to touch another phone to communicate with it has practical advantages in terms of privacy and security.
- **QR codes:** These are square symbols (Figure 18.1) that an app can read and go to a web page, play a song, display a Facebook button, or send a text.

Figure 18.1 A sample QR code

All the above devices and technologies create a confusing array of new options for marketers. After a decade or two we might know a few things about how marketing plays out on the desktop. With these devices marketers are facing an even more intensely dynamic and turbulent situation.

One thing that is clear is that mobile devices are very personal. They are increasingly becoming a fashion statement. They are also always on and always in the proximity of their user. As Shankar et al. (2010) point out, before mobile, the consumer entered the retailer's environment. Now the retailer can enter the consumer's personal environment. This implies that the rules of marketing on a smartphone will not be identical to the rules for desktops even though a smartphone is really just a small IP-enabled computer with a two-way radio. Surely there are privacy issues (Chapter 5) that are present in mobile technology that are not so salient when a consumer is on a traditional computer.

This access to the consumer may well be mediated by other channel players, however. If I am using Google Maps on my cell phone to find a restaurant, has the restaurant lost some of its power to Google? Other channel players include Facebook, Foursquare and Apple.

Three mobile segments

Following the tradition of Chapter 9, we will provide an overall segmentation scheme for mobile users. Our scheme will borrow the terminology of Shankar et al. (2010) and others cited in that paper:

- **Millennials:** These are younger, tech-savvy consumers who are digital natives without a long tradition of loyalty to brick-and-mortar stores. These traditional stores may find it hard to win over an individual from this group without help from that individual's (online) social network. The group is very prevalent in the entire world, especially Europe and the city states of Asia, and is beginning to drive the mobile agenda in North America as well. Along with social apps, music, gaming and other hedonic pursuits are migrating to these users' phones.
- **Road warriors:** These are business people using phones for utilitarian purposes such as scheduling and calendaring, email, and accessing company data while out in the field. They are tech savvy like the Millennials but can be easily identified by their Bluetooth earpieces.
- **Concerned parents:** This group uses its phones to stay in touch with the first group! They may or may not be able to send or receive a text message, and often need help from the first group to make things work. They

do have a lot of spending power, however, and are typically a key segment for most of the economy. Reaching them will require simple-to-use and -learn applications that have an immediate and obvious benefit.

All three groups are increasingly using mobile in a retailing context. Traditionally, it is the consumer who enters the retailer's space. With mobile, we see this tradition upended as the retailer can enter the very personal space of the consumer's mobile phone. Since the main competitive advantage for a retailer is location, clearly the notion of mobile location-based services suggests that retailing will be disrupted by this technology for years to come (Shankar et al., 2010).

 QUESTIONS AND EXERCISES

1 Have you personally observed any "mobile marketing"? How did it work out for you? Were you satisfied with the outcome?
2 What are some legal implications of mobile marketing? What are some potential ethical issues that might emerge?
3 What is the potential for "mobile coupons" to be sent directly to the consumer's phone? How would you manage a mobile coupon campaign?
4 In your opinion, how is marketing on a smartphone different than marketing on a computer?

 REFERENCES

Mace, M. (2006), "European vs. American mobile phone use," *Mobile Opportunity* [blog], accessed October 16, 2008 at http://mobileopportunity.blogspot.com/2006/09/european-vs-america n-mobile-phone-use.html.

Shankar, V., A. Venkatesh, C.F. Hofacker and P. Naik (2010), "Mobile marketing in the retailing environment: Current insights and future research avenues," *Journal of Interactive Marketing*, **24** (2), 111–20.

Wikipedia (2018), "List of countries by number of mobile phones in use," accessed February 8, 2018 at http://en.wikipedia.org/wiki/List_of_countries_by_number_of_mobile_phones_ in_use.

19
Selling strategy

It is the task of the e-tailer to add value as the consumer works through the different steps of problem solving discussed in Chapters 15 and 16. Compelling product descriptions and appealing images can initiate the problem recognition stage. Websites can facilitate search and evaluation using product comparison tools. Fulfillment strategy requires that the levels of pre- and post-purchasing support match consumer expectations. Trustworthiness in service expectations can be signaled through the use of guarantees. To this list we now add another series of strategies that we can employ in online retailing. Much of what you have already learned in the Basic Marketing course comes into play in this chapter. We talk about segmentation and products, about pricing, branding, competition and relationships. Of course, each of these will be discussed in a digital context.

Virtual segments

A segment is a relatively homogeneous group of consumers who react to a marketing action in a similar manner. In other words, the individuals within the group have similar tastes and preferences, and tend to react similarly to our offering. As an example, consider product preference. Some music fans enjoy hip hop, others might purchase country albums, and others listen to alternative. We might extend this notion and define a virtual segment as a set of consumers with similar tastes who have a low geographical density. Since there is low geographical density, we cannot justify reaching them using a traditional retailing channel. There are simply not enough of them in the same place to justify the expense of a store, a store that has to be cleaned, heated and cooled, protected, staffed, insured, and so forth. If I am going to sell mainstream fashion, I will possibly have enough customers to pay for a store even in a small town. But if we try to appeal to more obscure tastes, it becomes more difficult to break even.

Let's think about the charts for a moment. We are used to thinking about the Top 10 songs for the week, or maybe the Top 100 songs of the year. But musical tastes, and tastes for many other self-expressive product categories, allow for many more possibilities than 100. Let's imagine the Top 1000, Top 10 000 or, pulling out all the stops, the Top 10 000 000 songs! Taking rankings deep into the tail of the popularity distribution is an idea summarized by the phrase the "long tail," coined by Chris Anderson in *Wired*, October, 2004. His phrase was in turn inspired by an earlier academic paper by Brynjolfsson, Hu and Smith (2003).

The logic of the long tail retail strategy is that instead of selling a small number of products to a large number of customers, we sell a large number of products where each one appeals only to a small number of customers. The long tail retail strategy is logically the opposite of the classic star system that has reigned in offline music, movies, books and other media – before long tails were possible, a small number of star products would gather almost all of the sales. But, if I don't have to pay for heating and cooling a store, I can afford a much larger assortment of items to sell and therefore better serve smaller and smaller segments. This is the essence of the marketing strategy of segmentation. The long tail strategy is especially applicable to digital products. We know that the costs of manipulating, copying and storing digital data are going down and down. Digital data include music, games, movies, books and other art forms, but, in fact, even items like clothing, jewelry and other easy-to-ship items are amenable to the long tail strategy.

The long tail approach is shown in Figure 19.1. The x-axis shows a list of products, with the most popular product on the left, the second most popular product next to it, and so on, until we reach the far right of the x-axis and we find niche products. The y-axis shows the sales (in dollars or euros, etc.) of each of the products. An offline retail establishment can afford to sell only the items in the left part of the distribution, while an online store can sell those plus the less popular items. Note that revenue is equal to the area under the curve, and that the actual tail on the right part of the figure extends

Figure 19.1 The long tail

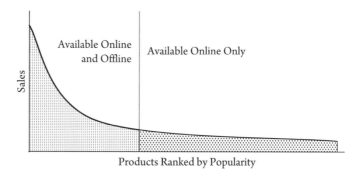

Available Online and Offline

Available Online Only

Sales

Products Ranked by Popularity

indefinitely off to the right, past the right margin of the page. The long tail strategy asserts that the area to the right of the distribution will be larger than the area to the left.

The exact shape of the figure matters a lot! If sales fall off slowly from left to right, it means that many sellers can enjoy substantial revenue. On the other hand, if the curve immediately falls off sharply, the situation is closer to "winner-take-all," a situation described in Brynjolfsson, McAfee and Cummings's (2014) book on what they call the "Second Machine Age."

Prices online

Economics classes often introduce the notion of pure competition. Pure competition occurs when there are many buyers and sellers, but specifically many sellers with the same commodity product available for the buyer. Pure competition also assumes low entry barriers on the part of sellers. Finally, it assumes perfect information, or in other words, that all sellers' prices can be easily discovered by buyers. To the extent to which buyers can easily discover all the sellers' prices, we say we have price transparency. Do these conditions remind you of anything? Doesn't all this sound like the online world? In the next paragraph, we explore why online competition seems to resemble pure competition. But for now, we should understand one thing – as marketers we better hope that online competition is not "pure," and here is why. Pure competition – especially the part that says consumers can easily learn every-body's prices – predicts that all prices from all sellers should quickly end up the same. And what price will all sellers have to charge? The theory predicts that all prices must fall to the level charged by the seller with the lowest costs. Ugh. That isn't marketing, that is just pure operational efficiency that ends up with all but one firm out of business.

Online, it is surely the case that anyone can throw an online storefront up, so it seems that we have many sellers and low entry barriers. While it is not clear that all consumers have perfect information online, it is fairly easy to search and to compare prices. You can even automate the process using shopbots. So, if I am looking for a particular book let's say, the competition is, to use a cliché, just a click away. Online retailing seems like it might be a perfect example of pure competition. To put this another way, described as above, online retailing is every marketer's worst nightmare. Oh, and it gets worse.

Customers are not dumb – they can figure out that online merchants have low costs. This is known as price imputation. In addition, there are ways that consumers can band together to drive prices down even further, using networking services such as Autobytel, which offers consumer purchase requests and marketing resources to car dealers and manufacturers and provides consumers with the information they need to purchase new and used cars.

Taking all these factors into account, it seems clear that we should predict the following: (1) prices should be lower online than offline; (2) price dispersion should be lower online than offline. These seem like two perfectly reasonable hypotheses. The only problem is that it appears they are both wrong. For example, Ancarani and Shankar (2004) compared books and DVDs online and offline. The picture is somewhat confused by the presence of shipping costs, but it seems clear from their data that books and CDs are not much cheaper online, if at all. There is also substantial price dispersion online. In other words, prices vary quite a bit from one online retailer to the next. But if the consumer can easily find a lower price, how can the more expensive site get away with it? It appears that online search costs and switching costs (remember the cliché, "only a click away"?) are more substantial than we might imagine. To rephrase slightly, retailing sites are fairly sticky (i.e., reluctant to change). And to put it yet another way, price sensitivity might be fairly low online. This view is bolstered by an estimate of price elasticity by Baye, Morgan and Scholten (2003). Those authors estimated Barnes & Noble's price elasticity at –4.0, which implies high price sensitivity. But Amazon's elasticity was a mere –0.5. Shoppers were willing to pay more to shop on Amazon's website.

Why aren't online prices lower than low?

Retailers have long known that convenience is king. Site owners have figured out how to make shopping easy. The consumer will pay for "easy." The sites themselves – like Amazon mentioned above – are branded service offerings that consumers actively seek out. It may be that anyone can toss up a site on the Internet and proceed to sell books, but consumers like Amazon and they stick with it.

We have already talked about the long tail strategy above. Online retailers can create vastly larger product assortments to sell than can offline retailers. This adds to the convenience of Internet shopping, and lets the e-tailer serve small segments around the world fairly efficiently.

How else can retailers enhance online convenience? One way is to offer supplementary services (see Chapter 2), both before and after the sale. Before the sale they can employ recommendor systems. Ansari, Essegaier and Kohli

(2000) note that there are five different types of recommendor systems. These are based on the following:

- **Collaborative filters:** A coefficient of agreement can be computed between the purchases of any two customers. The more agreement between the purchases, the more likely the consumers' tastes are similar. The store software can then show them or recommend to them options based on other customers with whom they have a very high coefficient of agreement.
- **Content filters:** You can ask the consumer to express what she or he likes, and then have the store software show them items they have told you they will like, or present items while highlighting product attributes they have told you are important.
- **Purchase history:** Software can make recommendations based on the customer's previous choices.
- **Individual characteristics:** A program might use demographic or geographic information to predict what the visitor will like. In effect, the program attempts to segment the incoming customer based on some knowledge of who they are. This knowledge might come from their Internet domain name (for example, the hypothetical names cable-co. net, bigu.edu or buongiorno.it might provide clues as to who is at the other end of the connection), from their sales record (Mr. vs Ms.) or their location (you can do a "reverse IP lookup", i.e., figure out approximately where their IP address is located).
- **Expert judgment:** A human can function behind the scenes and make expert recommendations. An expert, human or otherwise, is especially useful when we are choosing within a utilitarian product category.

The offline retailer has the possible advantage of a skilled salesperson recommending the perfect product to the customer. Creating a long-term relationship with the customer by offering good recommendations that make that customer happy is a classic marketing strategy used by generations of retailers. Online we attempt to do the same thing, usually with software, although expert judgment is an exception that uses human brain power behind the scenes instead of computing power.

The above five types of recommendor systems are only going to be useful under certain conditions (Hanson and Kalyanam, 2007 talk about these conditions on p. 308). First, the customer lifetime value (CLV is discussed in Chapter 7) of individual customers must be sufficiently large to justify the expense of the recommendor system. Next, the consumer must actually need or at least appreciate some kind of help. For utilitarian products, help

Figure 19.2 In cross-selling we sell a second product (B) and in up-selling we sell an improved version (A′) of the original product

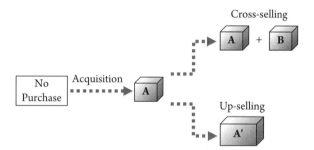

is often needed with complex product attributes (how many megapixels do I really need?). For hedonic products, help is often needed with qualitative or subjective product attributes (I wonder if I am going to like this DVD?).

The retailer can also add value to the purchase after the sale. They can offer opt-in newsletters. They can host a virtual community to encourage consumers to help each other. They can also execute cross-selling and up-selling, visualized in Figure 19.2.

In Figure 19.2, assume that a customer has been acquired and has chosen product A. The retailer can implement complementary good cross-linking, in much the same way that a savvy salesperson might suggest a tie to go along with a chosen shirt. This is called cross-selling and in the figure, B represents the complementary good. The retailer may also offer a substitute for A, call it A′, where A′ is a higher-margin item.

Price transparency on the Internet cuts both ways. Just as the consumer can check out prices on the competition's website, so can the e-tailer. This is known as competitive scanning. Because it is so easy to change prices online (this is known as having low menu costs), the online retailer can tune prices minute by minute. There is also the possibility of price discrimination, which simply means charging different prices to different customers. Ordinarily, you want to try to discriminate by lowering your prices only to price-sensitive customers. This is the basic idea behind coupons. The hard part is trying to figure out who is price sensitive and who is not. You can estimate price sensitivity from the customer's previous purchases from you, from their IP address or domain name, or from other information.

? **QUESTIONS AND EXERCISES**

1 We should review some economic terminology that comes into play in this chapter. Define the following:
   (a) price dispersion;

    (b)   price sensitivity;

    (c)   price elasticity;

    (d)   complementary good.

2 Explain why, under perfect competition, price dispersion is expected to be low.

3 Visit a retail website not mentioned in this chapter. Document which of the strategies included in the chapter are being used by the retailer.

4 Pick out a specific model of camera. If you prefer, use a different product category, but pick a very specific model. Now, go online and find at least ten sites that sell the model you picked. Record the prices for that model for the ten sites. Explain in marketing terms what you have observed with this experiment.

 REFERENCES

Ancarani, F. and V. Shankar (2004), "Price levels and price dispersion within and across multiple retailer types: Further evidence and extension," *Journal of the Academy of Marketing Science*, **32** (2), 176–87.

Anderson, C. (2004), "The long tail," *Wired*, October, accessed February 6, 2018 at https://www.wired.com/2004/10/tail/.

Ansari, A., S. Essegaier and R. Kohli (2000), "Internet recommendation systems," *Journal of Marketing Research*, **37** (3), 363–75.

Baye, M.R., J. Morgan and P. Scholten (2003), "The value of information in an online consumer market," *Journal of Public Policy & Marketing*, **22** (1), 17–25.

Brynjolfsson, E., Y. Hu and M.D. Smith (2003), "Consumer surplus in the digital economy: Estimating the value of increased product variety at online booksellers," *Management Science*, **49** (11), 1580–96.

Brynjolfsson, E., A. McAfee and J. Cummings (2014), *The Second Machine Age: Work, Progress, and Prosperity in a Time of Brilliant Technologies*, New York: W.W. Norton & Company.

Hanson, W. and K. Kalyanam (2007), *Internet Marketing and E-Commerce*, Mason, OH: Thomson South-Western.

20
Hubs and auctions

In this chapter, we talk about business-to-business electronic hubs, and look at the many types of hubs that exist. Most e-hubs do not use list pricing, but instead use some form of dynamic pricing mechanism, most commonly, the auction. We therefore want to compare and contrast list prices with auctions, and take a look at the many different types of auctions. We wrap up the chapter with a brief discussion of XML – a way to automate bidding and transaction execution.

Hubs or e-marketplaces

An e-hub, or e-marketplace, is a virtual platform that functions as a hub or portal for electronic business-to-business (B2B) transactions. There are quite a few "flavors" of e-hubs, and in fact we can organize the world of e-hubs many different ways (see Kaplan and Sawhney, 2000). To start, we may wish to organize e-hubs by who owns them. Some of them are independent exchanges owned by third parties (e.g., FreeMarkets, Intercontinental Exchange). In this context, a third party is simply someone other than the buyer or seller. Other types of e-hubs are industry consortia set up jointly by key industry players or trade associations (e.g., Elemica – chemicals, Covisint – auto, Exostar – aerospace, Quadrem – supply chain services). Finally, we have e-hubs that operate under private ownership (call them private e-hubs). These are typically "invitation-only" websites, or in other words, extranets. For example, Cisco runs an e-hub for its customers, while Wal-Mart runs an e-hub called Retail Link for its suppliers.

We can also organize e-hubs by the way they specialize. We see e-hubs that focus on a particular industry or market (e.g., Global Healthcare Exchange, ChemConnect). We can term these vertical e-hubs. Other e-hubs focus on the same business process across different industries (e.g., Employease). A good name for these is horizontal e-hubs.

There is a third way to think about e-hubs. In addition to categorizing them by who owns them or their mode of specialization, we might think about who benefits from the e-hub. Some e-hubs are fairly neutral but others are biased either in favor of the buyer(s) or in favor of the seller(s). The way you can detect bias is by noting which side of the market is "pooled" or "aggregated." An e-hub that favors sellers tries to reduce competition among sellers, pooling (aggregating) them and allowing them to speak with one voice while attempting to get as many independent buyers into the process as possible (e.g., Ingram Micro, e-Chemicals). We call these forward aggregators as the auction is running in the usual (forward) direction, with would-be buyers bidding against each other. On the other hand, other e-hubs function as reverse aggregators, where the buyer or buyers speak with one voice, but there are lots of independent sellers trying to undercut, or underbid, each other (e.g., Network FOB, FreeMarkets, Wal-Mart). Some e-hubs are neither forward aggregators nor reverse aggregators. We can call that sort of neutral hub an exchange (e.g., NASDAQ, London Stock Exchange).

Fixed prices vs dynamic prices

Though they might seem completely normal to you, fixed prices (or list prices) are a relatively recent phenomenon in human history, emerging only in the nineteenth century. Before that, prices tended to be much more dynamic, changing from moment to moment or customer to customer. In today's world, there are six common dynamic pricing models:

- **Yield management:** This pricing method is used to clear a market for perishable items such as airline seats, hotel rooms or concert tickets. The basic logic is to compare your available inventory with historical data. If you are running ahead of the historical norm (i.e., there are fewer seats left than usual), you raise the price, and if you are running behind the norm (there are more seats left than is normally the case) you lower the price.
- **Couponing:** Couponing is a classic sales promotion tool and also a longstanding price discrimination mechanism. People with a bit more time than money, or who are otherwise more price sensitive or price conscious, spend the time necessary to deal with coupons. The other segment – the less price-sensitive segment – doesn't bother. Voila! Two segments, two prices. We have thus achieved price discrimination.
- **Location pricing:** This is a new technique, especially applicable to mobile interactions (Chapter 18) where price can be based on the location of the consumer.
- **Volume pricing:** Sometimes price is based on use, such as car insurance. Frequent-flyer programs can be thought of as an attempt to reduce the cost, or at least add to the benefits, for the high-use segment. Volume

discounts are a very common form of price discrimination used in B2B transactions.

- **Personalization:** This is a generic term that simply refers to any price discrimination mechanism that operates at the level of the individual.
- **Auctions:** The auction is the type of dynamic pricing that is growing fastest in the online world. In the section that follows, we will delve into B2B auctions, but business-to-consumer (B2C) and consumer-to-consumer (C2C) auctions most certainly exist and have become quite popular. In fact, to illustrate auctions we begin by discussing eBay.

Auctions

Why are auctions so popular online? Before we talk about eBay and its rapid rise, let's back up a bit and talk about classic offline retailing. One of the ways that goods retailers benefit both manufacturers and consumers is by providing a matching function. When I go the grocery store and buy a particular box of cereal, the store has helped match me and the cereal maker, or connect us. Different manufacturers have different offerings and different consumers have different tastes. The retailer enables the right seller to match up with the right buyer.

My supermarket is different from eBay, however, in two key ways. First, retailers, whether they be offline or online, generally take title to the merchandise. They buy from the manufacturer and then resell. eBay plays a more neutral, broker-like role, not taking title to anything. Second, and more obviously, eBay's matching function is achieved by software, not by aisles and shelves. Both these differences lead to vastly more flexibility, and more flexibility in the matching function allows the consumer to better match his or her preferences with an offering. Think of how easy it is to search and sort with the help of software. Likewise, the flexibility of eBay allows the seller to better connect with a specific, small group of consumers, possibly only one consumer, and serve that individual or group.

Thus, we could say that eBay earns revenue from providing a matching function, but instead, let's refer to it as providing a "network connection" from one group (buyers) to another group (sellers). Using Internet terminology highlights why eBay is a prototypical Internet business, and it also highlights why the growth of the Internet computer network has boosted the popularity of auctions. The two – the Net and the auction – fit together pretty well. Internet auctions allow for flexible matching or connectivity.

The authors Pinker, Seidmann and Vakrat (2003) have listed a set of conditions that must hold for an auction to be the best-selling choice as compared to a fixed price: (1) the seller doesn't know what to charge; (2) buyer reservation prices vary; (3) we have rare or unique goods; or (4) we have expensive goods. In general, auctions are a very effective price discovery mechanism. It makes sense then to use an auction when the seller doesn't know what to charge. This might be because they have not done any research on the best price, or simply because buyers vary so much in their valuation of the product that it is hard to predict the reaction of any particular buyer, research or not. When buyers vary greatly in their reservation price (willingness-to-pay), we can benefit from implementing price discrimination such that those who are willing to pay more are allowed to come to the front of the buying line. An auction allows this to happen by rewarding higher bidders. It is also the case that when we have rare or unique goods to sell, we are more likely to be ignorant about buyers' willingness-to-pay.

Another point made by Pinker et al. (2003) is that auctions generally work best with expensive goods, because auctions tend to have high transaction costs. For inspiration in understanding this point, let's think about an art auction physically taking place in New York or London. Given the costs involved in running an auction, it is unlikely that Sotheby's or Christie's are going to bother to auction somebody's used bicycle. But eBay uses the "Internetwork" and software to automate the transaction between the buyer and the seller. These days selling a potato chip that has an image of your favorite professor on it can even be sold at auction! Well, maybe that's a bad example.

Networked software adds a whole set of benefits to auctions. For example, you can create complex auctions involving multiunit sales, or conditional bidding on bundles. To illustrate conditional bidding, think about a trucker's auction site where owners of rigs bid on the right to haul loads from one city to another. If I haul a load from Tallahassee to Wichita, it would surely be more profitable not to have to come back home with an empty truck. So, I can bid $1000 on the Tallahassee–Wichita run, bid $1000 on a Wichita–Tallahassee load, but specify that unless I win both bids, I don't want either job. Keeping track of millions of combinations and conditional relationships among bids is something that computers can do without even breaking a silicon sweat.

No chapter on auctions would be complete without at least a look at the downside to auctions. Some of the following are discussed in the book by Laudon and Traver (2003). Auctions:

- work against relationships since they emphasize price not service;
- delay consumption relative to fixed price outlets;
- force parties into monitoring each other or blindly trusting; and
- the buyer rather than the seller typically pays fulfillment costs including packing, shipping and insurance.

Categories of auctions

There are many types of auctions, and new types of auctions are being invented every year. To get a handle on the different kinds of auctions, we start by thinking about how to categorize them. Then we will cover a few classic auction formats. We can categorize auctions on the basis of the following features:

- **Number of sellers and buyers:** Just as e-hubs can be categorized as biased, so can auctions. For example, if there is only one seller but lots of buyers bidding against each other, this tends to work in favor of the seller. Conversely, a single buyer entertaining bids from many sellers is the buyer's dream situation.
- **Reverse vs forward auctions:** A forward auction is the better-known type, with a set of buyers doing the bidding against each other. In a reverse auction, also known as a procurement auction, the sellers are doing the bidding.
- **Open vs closed bids:** Some auctions use sealed bids (which are closed) so that no bidder knows what any other bidder has bid, while in other auctions there is bidding transparency.
- **Single or multiple bid rounds:** The winner can be declared after a single bid from all interested participants, or, typically after revealing all the bids, some types of auctions allow the bidding to continue with a second round of bidding, or more.
- **Ascending or descending prices:** The classic example of an auction that we see on TV or in the movies has prices ascending as a result of the bidding process. The auctioneer instead can start with a high price, and slowly reduce it. The first buyer to (electronically or literally) shout out wins the auction.
- **Single unit or multiple units:** Auctions in which lots of items are sold simultaneously are common online. A seller might have a dozen items of the same make and model available, and has put all of them up for auction at once.
- **Uniform or discriminatory price rules:** In multiple unit auctions, we could see all winners pay the same amount (uniform price rule), or we might have all winners pay whatever they last bid (discriminatory price rule).

Here are some fairly classic types of auctions:

- **English or ascending auction:** Here the price starts low and goes up. From the sellers' point of view, the disadvantage of this auction is that the winner could walk away with the item at a lower price than his or her maximum willingness-to-pay.
- **Dutch or descending auction:** In this case the price starts high and goes down until someone claims the item.
- **Yankee multiunit, ascending price auction:** Buyers bid on both quantity and price. This auction type has a discriminatory price rule such that all winners pay their bid price.
- **Name your own price auction:** Here there is a single round utilizing sealed bids. This is the priceline mechanism.
- **Vickrey auction:** The Vickrey auction has the peculiar property that the winner does not have to pay what he or she bid. Instead, the winner must pay what the second highest bidder bid. That's right – the winner pays the second highest bid price. As Heyman, Orhun and Ariely (2004) explain, this encourages the bidder to bid exactly what he or she thinks the offering is worth. If you bid under your willingness-to-pay, you might lose at a price that in fact you were willing to pay. If you bid over your willingness-to-pay, you might end up overpaying. Note that Google AdWords uses Vickrey auction rules.
- **Dutch-Internet multiunit ascending price auction:** eBay uses these rules, but note that this auction is misnamed! Technically, it is an English auction, not a Dutch auction. It is unclear why eBay calls it a Dutch auction, but that is just what they call it. In any case, there is a uniform price rule such that the lowest successful price determines the price for all winners.

Auctions can be implemented electronically with little human intervention. The cost benefit of automating buying and selling is not lost on businesses. Even the B2B pre-auction search function has recently been automated using a new language called XML.

XML

XML refers to Extensible Markup Language. This lets companies design their own markups or tags, which thereby facilitates search and reduces the cost of specification when there is a complex product description. HTML (Chapter 11) was designed for rendering on a browser for humans to see and read. An XML tag can do that if needed, but its main use is in machine-to-machine communication. For example, a buying firm might have a software agent looking at a set of online catalogs, and reporting back to management which deal is the best option available on the Internet. To give an example here, suppose a donut firm wants to search for sources of jam. Searching using a website based on HTML (let's say, like Google's), would possibly result in someone having to wade through a lot of entries about traffic jams! But a catalog firm can create a DTD (Document Type Definition) in which it defines a series of markups that might look like the following:

```
<jam>
<price>12.99</price>
<flavor>grape</flavor>
</jam>
```

It can then share this markup and others with suppliers and catalogers. If the industry buys in to these markup definitions, everybody can then search more effectively and automatically. The Open Buying on the Internet (OBI) consortium helps ensure that buyers' and sellers' XML tags are all interoperable.

QUESTIONS AND EXERCISES

1 Be prepared to define:
   (a) reservation price;
   (b) liquidity;
   (c) willingness-to-pay;
   (d) price discovery.
2 Why is there only one eBay, instead of lots of smaller companies that all compete in the field of C2C auctions?
3 In the text for this chapter, you saw some sample XML markups for a hypothetical donut maker wanting to more easily find "jam" catalog items. Work up some XML markups for a tropical fish retailer who wants to help buyers locate different species of fish.
4 If auctions work against B2B relationships, what sorts of business goods or services are most likely to be sold using auctions?
5 Uber uses dynamic prices such that the price of a ride might be very expensive on a Saturday night but relatively inexpensive on a Wednesday afternoon. Is this ethical? You might wish to refer to some of the ideas in Chapter 5 in your answer.

REFERENCES

Heyman, J.E., Y. Orhun and D. Ariely (2004), "Auction fever: The effects of opponents and quasi-endowment on product valuations," *Journal of Interactive Marketing*, **18** (4), 7–21.

Kaplan, S.N. and M. Sawhney (2000), "E-hubs: The new B2B marketplaces," *Harvard Business Review*, **78** (3), 97–103.

Laudon, K.C. and C.G. Traver (2003), *E-Commerce. Business, Technology, Society*, Boston, MA: Pearson.

Pinker, E.J., A. Seidmann and Y. Vakrat (2003), "Managing online auctions: Current business and research issues," *Management Science*, **49** (11), 1457–84.

21

Information versus inventory

In this chapter, we return to business-to-business (B2B) marketing and discuss supply chain management in the context of digital networks like the Internet. We start off with an explanation of what we mean by the supply chain and why supply chains are important. We then turn to the key issue of how firms manage the inventory that works its way down the supply chain. The Internet and related technologies have allowed firms to better manage this inventory by sending more information up the supply chain. Most of the latter part of this chapter addresses the idea of why excess inventory is not desirable and why we want to reduce it. We want whatever inventory is in the supply chain to keep moving. In fact, "inventory management" really means "inventory reduction." In other words, as marketers we want our supply chain to be lean. If our customers are other businesses, we can surmise that they too seek leanness and we should strive to help them achieve it. Technology gets us there by "replacing" inventory moving down the supply chain with information moving up the supply chain.

The supply chain

> [A supply chain is] a set of three or more entities (organizations or individuals) involved in the upstream and downstream flows of products, services, finances, and/or information from a source to a customer.

Mentzer et al. (2001, p. 4), whose definition appears above, have pointed to the growing importance of the supply chain in marketing and in business in general. As we learned in Chapter 8, digital networks can encourage outsourcing. This means that vertical processes that were formerly owned by a single firm might now involve numerous firms. Where, previously, competition played out according to a firm vs firm structure, competition has switched today to supply chain vs supply chain. Firms within the same supply chain work on new ways to collaborate so that the whole supply chain can compete better. Much of this new collaboration involves digital communication.

Let's think about some ways that firms can work together. The upstream firm (the selling firm) can take into account the needs of the downstream firm (the buying firm) and design goods, including packaging, to match those needs. The selling firm's new product development process can take into account factors such as the buying firm's warehouses, how big they are and how they are structured, where they are located, what size vehicles are ideal for them and how the loading facilities work. In terms of services, the upstream firm can customize its hiring and service management to eliminate headaches that afflict its downstream partner.

The downstream firm can help the upstream firm by revealing sensitive information to it. No information is more sensitive than how a company is doing with its own customers. But if I tell my suppliers what my customers want, how much they are buying, what my production schedules look like, what demand for my products looks like and what my inventory levels are, this helps my supplier help me. If I can work up enough trust, I might even let my supplier see inside my cash registers! Obviously, revealing my point-of-sale information requires a lot of trust. But, as discussed in Chapter 8, communication can lead to increased trust, and communicating inexpensively via digital networks has now become quite feasible. If we can achieve a sufficient level of trust, and allow more information to flow upstream, the more efficient the supply chain can be.

I communicate with my upstream suppliers via an extranet. An extranet allows me to execute procurement processes, maintain quality and trustful supplier relations, and buy raw materials, consulting help and other goods and services.

Internally within my company I communicate via an intranet (Chapter 6). This helps me keep my internal operations efficient, process materials and keep tabs on manufacturing and packaging, and perform many other functions more efficiently.

Downstream, I might communicate either via an extranet (if my customers are other businesses, like retailers) or the Internet (if my customers are ordinary consumers or end users).

Now we arrive at the central concept of this chapter. The more information that moves up the supply chain, the more efficient we can make the flow of material and services down the supply chain. Figure 21.1 gives the general idea, with the firm that we focus on in the middle, its upstream supplier on the left, and its downstream customer on the right.

Figure 21.1 A schematic diagram of a supply chain. Information moves up and goods and services move down the chain

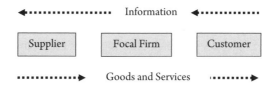

What we are going to do is to replace inventory with information. In other words, a more efficient supply chain has less supply in it, not more. In thinking about inventory, less is more! We address inventory reduction next.

Just-in-time inventory management

Pioneered by Toyota and other Japanese firms after World War II, the just-in-time (JIT) management philosophy has been widely imitated around the world. The essence of this philosophy is to reduce inventory and make production "leaner." Ideally, four outsourced tires should arrive at a Ford plant one instant before those tires are to be put on a new Ford Focus. To understand how we can pull that off, let's take a step back and flesh out the JIT philosophy. JIT emphasizes sole sourcing. Firms commit to a relationship with a partner and the two firms make reciprocal investments in technology.

In JIT, the management and marketing areas focus on relational exchange between supply chain partners, not on short-term profits based on the (opportunistically) highest transaction price. With JIT, the supplying and purchasing firms are in it together for the long term. JIT is quite consistent with the key notions behind B2B relationship marketing, the subject of Chapter 8. Supply chain partners therefore make a joint effort in continuous product improvement, and both invest in the relationship by making mirror-image investments in technology. Their production schedules become tightly knitted together. If these goals are met, the buying firm can trust the supplier enough to start reducing inventory levels and not worry about getting put "over a barrel." But why is having a low inventory good from a business or marketing point of view?

Models for inventory

To think about why big inventories are a bad idea, we are going to borrow a theory from management science known as the economic order quantity (EOQ) model of inventory (Anderson, Sweeney and Williams, 2003). The EOQ model focuses on the tradeoff between making smaller, more frequent orders versus having to hold more inventory. If we were to ask, "What is the total cost of dealing with inventory?" we could conveniently divide the answer into two different types of costs. First, we have what are known as holding costs. A firm's total holding cost is usually expressed as a percentage rate per year (say 25 percent). Holding costs might include:

- breakage, pilferage and other losses;
- the cost of capital tied up in the inventory;
- insurance for the inventory;
- costs of storage itself: lighting, heating, protecting, owning or leasing real estate; and
- loss of flexibility and product obsolescence.

The above list begins to inform us as to why holding lots of inventory is bad. Of all these, the lack of flexibility is probably the hardest to quantify, but it is also the most serious issue from a marketing point of view. If I have a huge pile of product X in my warehouse, I cannot change tactics and begin to sell product Y.

A second type of inventory costs is ordering costs. Total ordering cost is expressed not as a percentage of the inventory, but as a fixed amount. Let's pick $40 as an example. Thus, our firm might spend $40 each time it makes an order. Ordering costs include components such as:

- paperwork and purchasing department labor costs;
- coordination between buyer and seller; and
- order verification.

Presumably, a firm is going to decide how much inventory to hold based on the total of the two costs. Lowering your inventory reduces the holding cost, but requires more frequent smaller orders and thereby ups your ordering cost. These two types of costs obviously trade off against each other. But if we look carefully at the items listed under ordering costs, we see that an extranet can reduce each of them. With computer networks, even the phrase "paperwork" is an anachronism. Obviously, information, including ordering information, is less expensive and more flexible when it is digitized than when it appears on paper. Electronic networks reduce the various administrative and logistical issues, and the costs involved in coordinating many small orders. All that information flowing upstream in the supply chain knocks down the ordering costs and reduces how much the two firms have to spend in order to coordinate. To top it off, more frequent digital communication can contribute to an atmosphere of trust, enabling the buying firm to relax even in the face of small inventories.

Quality and inventory

We have presented a cost argument for reducing inventory as well as a strategy argument based on flexibility. Now we come to a third argument based on the fact that inventory can hide problems (Bozarth and Handfield, 2006 do a great job of describing this phenomenon). In the Ford example, where the four tires arrive an instant before being put on a new Focus, we note that if any of the four tires that Ford receives from its supplier has a problem, Ford gets stopped in its tracks. On the other hand, if Ford has a warehouse filled with a million tires, even if half of them are bad, it can keep going for weeks. Basically, reducing inventory exposes problems and creates opportunities for process improvement up and down the supply chain. Big inventories can hide, among other things:

- absenteeism or worker issues;
- insufficient or unreliable equipment; and
- quality issues.

To summarize, the JIT lean inventory philosophy works to reduce waste, lead times, setup times, queue lengths and lot sizes, while increasing strategic flexibility, productivity and quality.

Difficulties in supply chain automation

We now come to that part in the chapter where we mention the downside. It is not easy for two firms to integrate their technology. The firms have to choose their IT standards jointly. Most firms have a set of legacy systems that pre-date today's Internet Protocol-centric world. Tying two incompatible legacy systems together, or tying a legacy system to today's IP-based networks, can be quite a challenge. It can also be difficult to estimate what the costs of doing this will be, or for that matter, what the benefits will be. For example, how do we value "increased flexibility"? How much will we gain by uncovering quality problems we currently don't know we have? What's more, a return on the technology integration investment might take a long time. And there is also the question of opportunism. Despite these questions, firms are increasingly collaborating with technology, and sending more information up the supply chain so as to not have to send so much stuff down it.

> **? QUESTIONS AND EXERCISES**
>
> 1 What do we mean when we refer to vertical structure?
> 2 Assume you are the marketing manager for a firm that provides a small motor used in a robot that is in turn used on an assembly line to produce vacuum cleaners. How do you help your client become more profitable using digital networks?

3 Loss of marketing flexibility is presented in this chapter as a type of inventory "holding cost." What marketing issues arise with the loss of flexibility in inventory? In what sorts of industries is such flexibility especially critical?

 REFERENCES

Anderson, D.R., D.J. Sweeney and T.A. Williams (2003), *An Introduction to Management Science*, 10th edition, Mason, OH: Thomson/South-Western.

Bozarth, C.C. and R.B. Handfield (2006), *Introduction to Operations and Supply Chain Management*, Upper Saddle River, NJ: Pearson Prentice Hall.

Mentzer, J.T., W. DeWitt and J.S. Keebler et al. (2001), "Defining supply chain management," *Journal of Business Logistics*, **22** (2), 1–25.

Section IV

Digital networks as a connection service

The Internet is a network and networks are ideal for connecting things. Thus, we see a variety of new services designed to do just that – to connect individuals or groups. Frequently, such connections are impractical in the offline world, as is the case with the online auctions described in Section III. The focus of this section therefore is on goods or services that tend to exist only in digital form. We start with Chapter 22, which explains how companies can market such digital content, but then, in Chapter 23, we move on to discuss the situation in which it is customers rather than the firm itself who generate the content, as occurs on Twitter, to pick an example. As a second example, contemplate Hewlett-Packard. HP hosts a virtual community of users who help each other solve technical problems. Thus, HP connects consumers who have problems with other consumers who can solve those problems. In such a case, the community is actively co-creating value with HP and for HP. In Chapter 24, we go on to talk about the virtual community that produces this help, and other content. At this point, we specifically delve into social media (Chapter 25). Next, with the book nearly over, we take a step back and look at the "big picture" of digital marketing strategy (Chapter 26). Finally, in Chapter 27, we wrap up this section, and the book, with a tentative peek at the future of digital marketing.

22

Information products

In this chapter and the next we are going to talk about firms that sell content or information – that is, sites or apps where the primary attraction is the site or app itself, with no offline component to the firm's value proposition. Another way to describe this is by saying that the firm's business model relies on the site to serve as a vehicle to deliver content. This digital content serves as a product that might either resemble an information good, which is more passively consumed, or an information service, which requires more active co-production activity on the part of the consumer. For example, the Zillow real estate website service asks you to type in your address, at which point the site tells you the value of your home. The iTunes service allows you to download music files, which exist as a type of information good. The *Wall Street Journal* provides content for readers in the form of constantly changing online articles about business. Quicken helps users balance their checkbook. Google Docs lets users write and share documents. In all these cases, the website is supposed to be a source of revenue, not just an expense, and serves to deliver a purely digital product. It should be noted that even firms that are not strictly in the business of selling content often engage in content marketing to generate engagement on the part of consumers.

The focus of this chapter then is on information goods or services that are created or provided by the firm, while Chapter 23 will focus on sites where site users create such content. This chapter is organized around the following three building blocks of getting content used or seen: getting traffic to the site, keeping the traffic on the site, and getting the traffic back to the site. In the first section, investigating how to drive traffic to the site, we briefly review Chapter 14 on advertising and then go on to talk about three other topics: location, location, location. The second section, exploring how we keep that traffic on our site, will focus primarily on pricing and revenue, the latter obviously a key factor for success since a business without revenue is like, well, let's just say that the lesson of the 2001 dot-com crash was that actual revenue is a good idea. The third section is fairly brief but it will cover the important question of customer retention.

Getting them there

The topic of consumer search is covered in Chapter 16, while using advertising to drive traffic to a site is featured in Chapter 14. All the types of electronic advertising discussed in that chapter are applicable here, including SMS, email, banners, keyword search and sponsorship. We might add viral marketing to that list. Viral marketing enlists the visitor to help spread a message or an action that helps the firm. The transmission of word-of-mouth information through an online community, almost like a virus, is analyzed in Chapter 24.

The surest way to get people to your site is to give them something worth visiting. Search engine rankings – specifically, Google's PageRank algorithm – try to quantify the quality of a website by looking at the number of other sites, and the PageRank of those, that link to your site. Rather than bribe or browbeat other sites to link to yours, you might as well just hunker down and make your site a good site. Why fight this logic? The user has too much power. Give them what they want instead of trying to trick Google into giving you a high, but undeserved, PageRank. If people arrive on your site and instantly flee, what have you accomplished?

Now the definition of what constitutes a "good" site, as we learn in Chapter 9, depends on whether the audience is seeking hedonic or utilitarian benefits from your digital content. If the audience consists primarily of the former, good means "entertaining." If the latter, your digital content needs to be useful.

Driving traffic to your site should not be limited to online media. All the offline mass media, as well as offline public relations, can and should be considered in driving folks to your site. One very powerful technique is to combine offline and online methods. Your offline advertisements should always include your online address. This allows you to stretch your ad dollars as well as the space available to you. Interested viewers can go to the site, where the ad, in effect, continues.

The geography of the Internet

Returning to the online world, we might stop for a minute to think about the difficulty or ease of getting to your site. In the physical world, finding a target location depends on the layout of the neighborhood and how close we are to the target. Online, the distance between any two pages is defined by the total number of clicks that it takes to get from the one to the other. This is true within any particular site, as shown in Chapter 13, or overall, across the entire Internet. The Internet, therefore, has a sort of geography where travel time is measured in clicks. In recent times, under the rubric of a new field called network science, people have begun to study networks of all types, including author networks (who cites whom), food webs (which organisms dine off of which other organisms), co-ownership networks (who owns what with whom), neural networks (which brain cells are connected to which others), protein networks (which proteins interact with which others), text messaging networks (who texts whom) and so on and so forth (Watts, 2004 summarizes these studies). All these networks share the property of self-organization. Network self-organization means that no one plans or designs the network; it generates its own organization from its own internal dynamic.

So, what is the internal dynamic of the Internet? How is it organized? What is its geography? In other words, on the Internet who links to whom and why? One simple hypothesis is that webmasters are more likely to link to a site the more incoming links there already are to that site. This notion is called preferential attachment. In effect, it creates a rich-get-richer phenomenon. While preferential attachment, as a theory, might be an oversimplification, it does explain many pertinent facts about the Internet, including phenomena such as the frequency distribution of links.

A simulated link distribution is given in Figure 22.1 for a network with 5 million pages. The number of incoming nodes for a page, in other words the number of pages that link to your page, is known as the in-degree. Do you recognize that the distribution of links follows a Power Law? The Power Law was discussed in Chapter 14.

Figure 22.1 A simulated frequency distribution for the number of links pointing to different pages

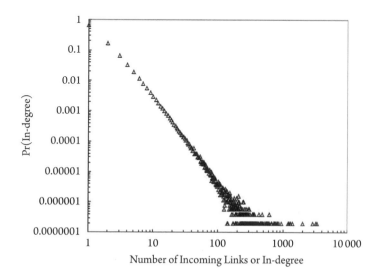

Preferential attachment can also explain the fact that the Internet is a small-world network. A small-world network is one in which the number of clicks to get from any randomly chosen point A to any other randomly chosen point B is smaller, on average, than might be expected. More specifically, the distance – or number of clicks – between any two randomly chosen nodes on a small-world network tends to be around log N, where N is the overall number of pages on the whole network. Two pages on a small-world network of size 100 tend to be around two clicks apart. If I scale up the network to 1000 pages, I have only added one extra click (log 1000 = 3) to the average voyage.

Keeping them there

The value of a content website depends on the difference between the "gives" and the "gets" of that website. Chapter 9 discusses some "gets," often called benefits, especially the section on hedonic and utilitarian visitors. Each of these two segments is looking for different types of benefits. That chapter also speaks to the "gives," especially non-monetary costs. We know that we want to create a website that provides scent at a distance – the visitor can tell that he or she will not have to burn much energy to find rich nuggets of information. We also know that ease of navigation will reduce the mental cost of using the website and keep people on the site.

Information goods that are more passively consumed tend to have different benefits from information services that are more actively, and interactively, co-produced. For the latter, flow is most important (see Chapter 9) but also immersion, which is a term applied to games, an important category of information product. For passively consumed information goods, such as movies or books, transportation is a key benefit (Van Laer and de Ruyter, 2010).

We now turn to visitors' monetary costs. How do we actually make money on a website? For some businesses, the website promotes a product, but for other businesses, such as Zillow and the *Wall Street Journal*, the site is the product.

As has been mentioned in the first paragraph of this chapter, a firm selling digital content of some kind can also be said to be in the business of selling an information product. Whether we call it digital content or information, these sorts of products have some peculiar properties compared to non-digital goods. For one thing, digital content is non-depletable – consuming information does not use it up. We can also say that, other than the server not having enough power to deal with the number of visitors, digital content is

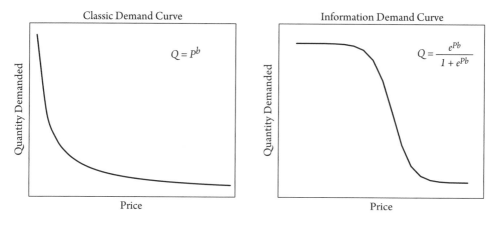

Figure 22.2 A comparison of the demand curve for goods or services with the demand curve for information

non-rivalrous in demand. Non-rivalrous demand means that one individual's consumption does not diminish another user's value or utility (Asvanund et al., 2004). In fact, an information product often exhibits increasing value with use by others, a topic covered under network externalities in Chapter 23.

Classic economic demand curves do not apply to information products. Classic demand curves go to infinity when the price goes to zero, as illustrated in Figure 22.2. But with digital content, once I have a copy of the product, there is no need to ever buy it again, since I can make my own copies if I need to. One sale per customer is the rule.

Another difference pertains to the cost function for digital goods. This function is basically flat, as illustrated in Figure 3.1 in Chapter 3 for email. Once the firm makes the first copy, it can make as many copies as it needs for a small amount of money. Obviously, making that first copy can be expensive – but the point here is that costs tend to be fixed and not variable. That means firms frequently want to use a penetration pricing strategy with as large an audience as possible to spread out that fixed cost. Another related strategy is the freemium model, in which a base or low-end version is free but the deluxe version costs money. Freemium works well in the presence of externalities.

The ease with which digital content can be manipulated leads to some important strategic advantages that accrue with such products. We can take our digital content and change it or process it in many different ways, including reproduction, storage, sorting, repurposing, bundling, unbundling, organization, distribution, packaging, reformatting, indexing, and connecting (Hofacker et al., 2007). All these activities, since they take place on a computer, are relatively easy and inexpensive to perform as compared to non-digital products. The bad news is that the ease of manipulating information also applies to the consumer. Once they get their hands on your file, they too can copy and share it with ease. It is no wonder that information companies are obsessed with legally protecting their goods and services from piracy, so much so that they often apply the name, intellectual property. The legal issues surrounding intellectual property are probed in Chapter 5.

Rather than seek legal redress, services marketing (Chapter 2) suggests that the owners of intellectual property should try to convert their information good into an information service, a technique called servitization. Such a strategy is consistent with what is often called the service-dominant logic of marketing (Vargo and Lusch, 2004). For example, rather than worrying about protecting its game software, the massively multiplayer online game (MMOG) *World of Warcraft* gives it away, and makes money on monthly subscriptions needed to play the game with others.

Now let's take one of those actions that a firm can easily perform on information and expand on the theme: bundling separate digital products into a single aggregate product. Unlike offline goods and services, information products can easily be logically combined and "repackaged" online by companies. The low cost of disk storage means that consumers, for their part, do not suffer any inventory inconveniences even for "large" bundles of information goods. Bundling is a tactic that yields higher profits whenever consumer valuations for two products are negatively correlated. To elaborate, if the bundle consists of two products, A and B, bundling adds to demand whenever A is liked by segment one more than segment two, while B is liked more by segment two than segment one. Bundling also allows you to achieve cost savings in production due to economies of scope, and to reduce variability in consumer valuation and thereby uncertainty in demand. Demand uncertainty mitigates against efficient pricing and so avoiding it helps the firm set optimal prices.

There are a variety of ways of creating revenue for content sites. A classic method is to make money from advertising. The website thereby becomes a platform for connecting two groups: content consumers and advertisers. Alternatively, some sites charge a viewer fee. Fees may be charged by the session, view, page, byte, search or by time. A related approach is to charge a subscription, defined as an "up-front" fee paid for access to the digital content.

Regardless of how the site generates income, it is necessary to get customers to the site, to keep them there, and then to get them back. We now turn to the last topic of the three.

Getting them back

How do we get visitors to come back to our site? Chapter 2 presents a model for repatronage that emphasizes two components: an affective component (expectations vs actual performance) and a cognitive component (costs vs benefits). We can now add one obvious way to get them to return: provide a benefit for doing so. We need to give them a reason to come back. We need to keep our content fresh and changing. The content on a website should have some sort of rhythm that matches management's target inter-visit cycle. If you want visitors to return weekly, your content turnover cycle should also be weekly. It is also important to use a mixture of push versus pull approaches. In addition to adding new material, you might have an opt-in email newsletter, or use a News or RSS feed to actively push material to the user's desktop.

Computer processing and disk storage are cheap compared to losing a potential customer. When they click on a link, or use their favorites or bookmark file, the link they hit should work! There is no reason that links should ever stop working. If the web page changes names, you should forward visitors to the new name automatically even if the visitor has used the old name. If the page is now obsolete or superseded, tell the visitor who lands on the old page by accident. Your own links to external sites should of course be checked frequently to make sure all of those are working.

? QUESTIONS AND EXERCISES

1 In network science, a network authority is a web page with a lot of incoming links and a network hub is a web page with a lot of outgoing links. If you are the webmaster of a content site, which type of page is better from the point of view of marketing?

2 This chapter refers to the distribution of links. Figure 22.1 shows the distribution of incoming links, or in-degree. We can also contemplate the out-degree distribution. So, how many sites are there (what is the probability of finding a site) with one outgoing link? Two? A thousand? Take a piece of paper and make a stab at what this distribution might look like. On the x-axis, put the number of outgoing links. On the y-axis, put the number of sites that exist with that many outgoing links. Sketch out the frequency distribution as some type of line or curve.

3 Here are the examples used in the beginning of this chapter: Zillow, iTunes, the *Wall Street Journal*, Quicken and Google Docs.
   (a) For each one, how do these firms generate revenue?
   (b) Are these firms offering an information good or an information service?

4 What is a demand function?

5 This chapter mentions service-dominant logic. How might a musical act transform itself from a

business that relies on the selling of a good (the DVD or the song), to one that relies on providing a service?

6 Compare the way that the Google News (news.google.com) website generates revenue and the way that the Fox News (www.foxnews.com) website generates revenue.

7 Do a competitive analysis comparing the two streaming services Pandora and Spotify.

 REFERENCES

Asvanund, A., K.B. Clay, R. Krishnan and M.D. Smith (2004), "An empirical analysis of network externalities in peer-to-peer music sharing networks," *Information Systems Research*, **15** (2), 155–74.

Hofacker, C.F., R.E. Goldsmith, E. Bridges and E. Swilley (2007), "E-services: A synthesis and research agenda," *Journal of Value Chain Management*, **1** (1), 13–44.

Van Laer, T. and K. de Ruyter (2010), "In stories we trust: How narrative apologies provide cover for competitive vulnerability after integrity-violating blog posts," *International Journal of Research in Marketing*, **27** (2), 164–74.

Vargo, S.L. and R.F. Lusch (2004), "Evolving to a new dominant logic for marketing," *Journal of Marketing*, **68** (1), 1–17.

Watts, D.J. (2004), "The 'new' science of networks," *Annual Review of Sociology*, **30**, 243–70.

23

User-generated content

It is time for us to distinguish between the physical world and the virtual world. The word virtual is often used to refer to what is digital and therefore exists only online – exists in the sense that software creates a sort of existence, but not in the sense that real-world objects like trees, or houses, or you and me, exist. The virtual world has the structure of a network, a self-organizing network where the geography is measured out in clicks. And what are networks really good at? What do they do really? That should be obvious: networks connect things.

So, we have come to the chapter that finally gets down to the purely virtual – that place in the economy that is now still less than a pair of decades old, where huge new firms have sprung up, firms whose business is essentially virtual and exists purely as a network phenomenon. Chapter 22 describes firm-generated content but in this chapter, the exposition concerns user-generated content. Many new online services, the most virtual firms out there, utilize user-generated content. For example, unlike a television network where professional directors create the shows and the audience watches, on YouTube the audience can both create and watch the content. Unlike the *Wall Street Journal*, sites like Blogger.com do not rely on professional writers. Instead, site visitors write the articles and site visitors read them. Unlike Wal-Mart where professional buyers buy merchandise and professional retailers sell it, on eBay, site visitors buy and sell their own merchandise.

It is interesting to stop and think about eBay (we thought about it in Chapter 20 covering auctions) as it's a prototypical example of an Internet company. Of course, we know that eBay is an online company, but so is Amazon. But Amazon still has to deal with the offline world. It needs to buy merchandise and to have warehouses. It needs to get the purchased items into people's houses and apartments. But eBay has none of these issues and touches the offline world even less than Amazon. So, how does eBay add value?

It basically adds value, and thereby earns revenue, by providing the benefits of a platform. This terminology – platform – is used by Eisenmann, Parker and

Van Alstyne (2007) and is very well chosen. A platform consists of several components often built from software and the architecture that specifies how the components work together. The platform also enforces some rules, both software and human, that add value. These rules are in the form of standards, protocols and policies. The components and the rules are designed to connect buyers and sellers.

So, we might compare Wal-Mart to Amazon and think that Amazon is more of an Internet company than Wal-Mart. But eBay is even more virtual than Amazon. eBay relies on user-generated content – in this case the content is physical and includes items like bicycles and rare coins and pictures of professors on potato chips. Sorry, that third example is not a very good one. eBay exhibits another property typical of the virtual world. eBay's market has strong externalities, and we proceed next by discussing those. Externalities are commonly seen on networks. It turns out, however, that there is more than one type of network and so we will also delve into the distinction between one-sided or peer-to-peer networks on the one hand, and two-sided networks on the other.

Externalities

> An externality is a benefit or harm experienced by party B due to the actions of party A, with no compensating payments between the parties.
> (Eisenmann, 2006)

While Eisenmann (2006) uses the word harm, we have been using the word costs (or "gives"). In the present case, the benefits are the content created by other users that I can enjoy as a user without directly paying for. For this reason, the externalities imply that the firm's value proposition is driven by users who co-create value.

Offline, externalities are sometimes negative. For example, when I drive a car, I create costs for others, others that I do not compensate, by adding congestion to the roads and parking lots, and pollution and potentially climate-changing exhaust to the air. Online, externalities are sometimes positive. As more and more people from my High School class join Facebook's platform, I get more and more benefit from the software. I do not compensate my classmates or anyone else, although, of course, I may ask to join their network of friends.

It is interesting to go back in time and think about the relatively simple networks that pre-date the Internet. A broadcast network, such as a radio station or collection of stations, does not tend to create any externalities. The benefit and hence the value of the network to the listener, does not particularly depend, either positively or negatively, on the number of other listeners. It is just a fixed constant, say a. The total benefit of such a network is therefore proportional to the number of listeners, that is, $n \times a$. This last relationship is sometimes called Sarnoff's Law, and it assumes that each of the n listeners experiences an equal benefit, that is, the constant a. To the owner of the network, the quantity $n \times a$ represents a simplified numerical estimate for the network's value.

Now let's think about the telephone network. In some sense, we can say that the phone network is analogous to a social network website like Facebook. In this case there definitely are positive externalities. The benefit to me of the phone network depends on the number of people I can connect with. Assuming that each of these people provide a benefit of b, and if there are n of them including myself, the benefit I get is $(n - 1) \times b$. The equation includes $n - 1$ rather than n because I don't experience any added benefit when I talk to myself. The total benefit of the network is then $n \times (n - 1) \times b$. If we work out the multiplication, we see a squared impact (n^2) rather than a linear impact. This equation is called Metcalfe's Law. If the network is more flexible than the phone network, we can perhaps create value from groupings of more than two people at a time. Assuming that all groups create the same amount of benefit – call it c – in that case the total number of possible groups is $2^n - 1$ and the total benefit comes to $(2^n - 1) \times c$. This last relationship is called Reed's Law. Note that the use of the constants a, b and c in the three laws represent a simplification of the actual situation. In reality, each new network node or group is surely not of equal value. Nevertheless, the three equations give us a sense for how externalities function in different types of networks.

Networks with externalities have the property that they are hard to get started. Why should I buy a phone if there is no one to talk to? Why would I bother to log on to Facebook if I was the only user on the platform? We can think of this as the chicken-and-egg problem of network services. Having said that, once a network with externalities manages to get started, we observe a virtuous growth cycle, illustrated in Figure 23.1. As it grows, since the benefit of the network has increased, it attracts more users. As those new users come on board, that causes the network to become even more valuable, thereby

Figure 23.1 The virtuous circle created when there are positive network externalities

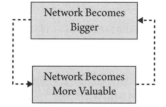

attracting even more new users. The appeal of that logic helped to fuel the dot-com craze that ended with the 2001 crash. Certainly, there were some huge winners and today their URLs are household names. Generally, networks with externalities tend to produce a winner-takes-all outcome. The number of winners is small, and the rest of the platforms fail due to a lack of critical mass.

Networks like the telephone system can be called a peer-to-peer network, since everyone on the network has the same power and plays the same roles. Anyone can make a connection and anyone can receive a connection. Next, we will talk about a different category of network where the users of the site fall into distinct groups. Instead of just connecting everybody with everybody else, the site connects people from one group to people from another group. Such networks are said to be multisided.

Two-sided networks

In a peer network, or perhaps we can call it a one-sided network, there are a set of homogeneous users who play different transient roles (Eisenmann, 2006). For example, in our telephone network, pretty much everybody plays the role of caller and callee from time to time. On Facebook, everybody writes profile information and everyone reads the profile information of others. There is a single market or population.

As Eisenmann (2006) explains, two-sided networks are different in that members always play the same role out of two available roles. On Hotmail, we can designate the two sides as users and advertisers. A Hotmail user will tend to stick to his or her own role and not switch groups and suddenly become an advertiser.

Parker and Van Alstyne (2005) define two-sidedness by noting that the network externalities cross from one side to the other. Advertisers on Hotmail (side A) benefit as the number of email users (side B) grows. We can call this type of effect a cross-externality.

According to Evans (2003), there are three different types of two-sided platforms. There are:

- **Market-makers:** Platforms that make a transaction of some sort between two groups (eBay, NASDAQ, match.com).
- **Audience-makers:** Platforms that connect viewers or users with advertisers (broadcast TV, Internet portals, Hotmail).
- **Demand-coordinators:** Platforms that enable different kinds of

activities (mobile phone network, debit card networks). The role of the platform is to make a physical or virtual network connection.

We should also note that three-sided networks, and above, can exist.

Revenue and pricing in two-sided networks

In a two-sided network, each side has its own "gives" and "gets" (or costs and benefits – see Chapter 2). These may be defined differently than the other side's gives and gets. To generate revenue, we need to figure out whether to charge both sides or to charge one side (call it, like Eisenmann, 2006, the money side) and subsidize the other side (the subsidy side). As with firm-generated content (Chapter 22), the charge can be a subscription or the charge can be based on the transactions executed between the two sides. Economic logic tells us that we should charge the side that is least price sensitive. It is important to take into account the cross-externalities when we are deciding upon a price, since if the price we charge side B reduces the number of participants from side B, this might make the platform less appealing to side A, and increase the price sensitivity of side A. Here as always, user costs are not necessarily strictly monetary. For example, being forced to view an ad can be considered part of the price a user might pay. This same analysis can be made of other marketing variables such as promotion and site design. The cross-side effects must be taken into account in managerial decision making.

Before we finish this chapter, let's spend some time contemplating one form of user-generated content, namely the "blog." A blog is short for "weblog," which is a chronologically organized site allowing users to express opinions, typically in the form of short essays.

HP and high-tech blogs

Here is a story that demonstrates that user-generated content is not just relevant to purely virtual companies. While blogs are a way for ordinary consumers to publish their own content, Hewlett-Packard (HP) developed an interesting marketing campaign around blogs. A few years back, HP developed a high-end gaming laptop called the Dragon. The model cost a whopping $5000 and had the latest and greatest laptop features. Despite the high quality of the machine, sales were very weak for the Dragon. HP decided to enlist the help of some popular tech blogs to stimulate interest in the product.

HP selected 31 different high-tech bloggers who had a large consumer following. As such, the blog owners were regarded as opinion leaders. HP contacted the owner of each blog and gave one Dragon laptop to each of them. The blog owner was not going to keep the laptop. Rather, the blog owner was to create a contest, however they saw fit, that would somehow involve consumers discussing the Dragon. Each contest's winner would be awarded the laptop at the end of 31 days. The promotion was dubbed "31 Days of the Dragon." The point was to get consumers engaged in discussing the Dragon. For HP and the blog owners this was a win–win situation: each would generate a lot of online chatter and PR.

The results were nothing less than amazing. Lots of consumers started blogging about the Dragon. This generated instant search engine benefits for HP, even though the blogs were not on the HP website. The large amount of chatter caused the top 50 links on Google's search engine result pages to display Dragon-related information whenever a consumer searched for HP. Over 380 000 links were created throughout the Web to the 31 different blogs. This market buzz increased sales by 85 percent for the Dragon laptop. The lesson is that even manufacturers can harness the power of user-generated content when they understand digital marketing.

QUESTIONS AND EXERCISES

1 Networks with externalities tend to create a single winner who "takes all." Why?
2 For each example, discuss how many sides there are to the network: one, two or three:
   (a) Google;
   (b) Mastercard;
   (c) Blogger.com;
   (d) YouTube;
   (e) Nintendo Game Boy;
   (f) *World of Warcraft*.
3 Network platforms frequently exhibit a chicken-and-egg problem. Until the network reaches a critical mass of users, no one wants to use it. What marketing strategies can we use to get a network up to and over a critical mass of users?

REFERENCES

Eisenmann, T.R. (2006), "Platform-mediated networks: Definitions and core concepts," *Harvard Business School Module Notes*, accessed January 15, 2018 at https://www.hbs.edu/faculty/Pages/item.aspx?num=33529.

Eisenmann, T., G. Parker and M. van Alstyne (2007), "Platform envelopment," unpublished working paper, Harvard Business School, accessed January 15, 2018 at www.hbs.edu/faculty/Publication%20Files/07-104.pdf.

Evans, D.S. (2003), "Some empirical aspects of multi-sided platform industries," *Review of Network Economics*, **2** (3), 191–209.

Parker, G. and M.W. van Alstyne (2005), "Two-sided network effects: A theory of information product design," *Management Science*, **51** (10), 1494–504.

24

Virtual communities

In many ways, the topic of the current chapter overlaps with Chapter 23 on user-generated content. In that chapter, we focus on the platform that enables the content, while in this chapter we are going to focus on the community of users generating the content. As such, we might begin by defining community. What follows is a fairly basic definition as might be proposed in a sociology text:

> A community is a group of people sharing cultural communalities and maintaining social interaction that is characterized by control, socialization and support.

The use of the word control in the definition implies that the community has norms, rules or laws that are enforced in some manner. The word socialization implies that the community shares some knowledge, traditions, rituals or values and that this information is imparted to new members who must learn it. Once learned, the members of the community can be said to share a culture, or at least a sub-culture. Culture is a set of thoughts, feelings and behaviors that we learn from other community members. Finally, the community offers support to its members, whether that be in the form of money, esteem, respect, fun or other benefits. Community membership comes with a sense of duty or obligation towards one's fellow community members.

So now that we have defined community, all that remains is that we define virtual community (VC):

> A virtual community is a community whose social interactions are generally mediated by software rather than occurring offline.

Why marketers care about virtual communities

Texas Instruments has created a platform where users of the firm's calculators can exchange tips and tricks. The Lonely Planet hosts a community of people who exchange travel information, suggesting out-of-the-way places and advising each other on which hotels have the best breakfast. Amazon sponsors a book-related community where readers provide reviews – some of which run many pages – of books they have read. These reviews can then be used by buyers who are evaluating alternative books. Kodak hosts a virtual community where users upload and comment on photographs, and exchange best practice ideas for taking pictures. Hewlett Packard sponsors a help forum where users help each other solve technical problems. KLM allows users to provide pointers to each other for when they visit China. Finally, Facebook has created a platform where I can easily read when my friend either praises or criticizes a brand I know.

In each of these cases a firm has set up a platform to enable and leverage user-generated content, and this content provides value to other customers. We can call such examples sponsored virtual communities. In effect, customers and the content they generate have been enlisted to provide some sort of marketing function. It is as if self-service is not enough. Not only will we ask you the customer to serve yourself, we are even going to ask you to provide benefits and help sell our products to other customers on our behalf! Of course, there are other virtual communities, among which Facebook comes to mind, that are not hosted for the purpose of using content for customer support, but the above examples certainly point out how powerful and useful a virtual community can be, as well as the general applicability of the idea.

Virtual community basics

In the above examples, the VC is organized around the sponsor. In addition, VCs are sometimes organized around interests (e.g., Sudopedia), around the practice of certain skills or specializations (e.g., PHP-Freelancers), shared fantasy (Eve Online), relationships (Facebook) or affinity (Yahoo! Groups covering religion, geography or politics).

According to Szmigin and Reppel (2004), virtual community bonding is rather important, and if successful, goes through several stages. At first, members may be barely aware that they are indeed a community. Eventually, the community may end up being an important component of members' identity, exhibiting what is called consciousness of kind (Muñiz and O'Guinn, 2001). Non-members begin to be not perceived as favorably as members. Sometimes this can get out of hand when brand community members go overboard and make the leap from advocates to badvocates. As the interconnected relationships within the community grow stronger, the community may come together to support its members as a moral responsibility. Often communities, online or offline, develop rituals.

One difficult aspect of nurturing the bonding process is that the hosting firm cannot manipulate the community with anything resembling a heavy hand. In fact, the bonding process requires that the firm relinquish control. Bonding has to come from within the community. The level of control to exercise always represents a challenging decision. One obvious control question is this: do we censor those in the community who attack our product?

As the community matures, it creates social capital. Following Bauer and Grether (2002):

> Social capital is a resource consisting of the network of social connections that can be drawn upon by individuals, or the firm.

As social capital grows, the basis for trust is created, and as described above, bonding takes place. Assuming all goes well and a VC takes off, there are many potential benefits that can accrue to the hosting firm (Porter, 2004):

- increased sales;
- more effective market segmentation;
- increased website traffic;
- a stronger brand;
- advertising and transaction fee revenue;
- improved product support and service recovery; and
- positive word-of-mouth.

This last benefit – word-of-mouth – has been studied in offline communities long before the Internet. It is known that consumer word-of-mouth can be much more powerful than company activities (Villanueva, Yoo and Hanssens, 2008) in terms of influencing consumer attitudes and behaviors. Consumer brand postings in the form of recommendations and product reviews can be very influential. What's worse for marketers is when a service mistake or product failure leads to negative word-of-mouth. Unlike just a few years ago, now when a consumer complains there may be hundreds of Facebook friends who hear them.

VCs provide a medium across which information can travel. This brings up the topic of viral marketing, where the community itself transmits the marketing information without any effort on the part of the firm. For example, the first free email program, Hotmail, included a trailer after each email that simply said: "Get your private, free email at http://www.hotmail.com." As each user joined Hotmail, they would naturally begin sending their usual emails to their friends and acquaintances. Each of these individuals would see the message at the bottom of the email, some of them would become Hotmail users, and the cycle would repeat in an expanding pattern of users.

Montgomery (2001) has noted that the classic Bass (1969) model can be used to track the viral transmission of information through a VC. In the Bass model, the people who have not yet become users of a new service like Hotmail are influenced by two different forces. There is the coefficient of innovation and the coefficient of imitation. The former coefficient quantifies the tendency for people to try a new service regardless of how many other people are, or are not, using it. The latter quantifies the importance of following the crowd. This model can be used to predict the peak conversion time and the overall conversion probability to a new online service.

Much of the benefits of a VC apply in the post-purchase time period where we can add value to the purchase. VCs can help with advice as to best practices, with new uses of the product, suggest new product ideas, give feedback on the current product portfolio, provide technical help and work to improve coordination between customers and the firm in many ways.

How to nurture contributions

Software can facilitate community processes while reducing costs in several ways, as described by O'Reilly (2005). (I believe Tim O'Reilly was the first analyst to use the phrase Web 2.0.) First, the software should default to "share." Sharing should occur without any action taken by the user. The software and the architecture of the platform should be designed for participation. VCs exhibit an onion-like property: there is a small core of people who create most of the content. In fact, we once again see the operation of a Power Law as mentioned in Chapter 14. In this case, the distribution of community contributions per individual also takes the form of a Power Law. The core content-producing folks need to be well supported and there needs to be an extension mechanism by which others can contribute as well. Finally, the platform should set conditions such that generating utility for the individual creates collective value for the group as a by-product. These actions can nurture community growth.

Chapter 23 on user-generated content points out that online externalities tend to be positive. Perhaps this is an overgeneralization. Certainly, there can be negative externalities. For example, as the VC grows ever larger, it generates more content, or conversation. At some point the amount of content generated might produce information overload, or otherwise end up being too much for members to handle. In the case of information overload, decision making actually gets worse with additional information. Here is where well-written software, or a human editor or moderator, can help. As in any other situation the user will contemplate the "gives" versus the "gets," and those costs, whether they be financial or otherwise, are weighed against the benefits. Software, or a firm employee, can reduce the mental costs needed to wade through more content produced as the VC becomes larger and larger by offering filtering, organizing, sorting and searching options as well as mechanisms that condense or summarize the community content.

QUESTIONS AND EXERCISES

1 Pick a social networking website that you are familiar with. This might include Facebook, YouTube, Google+, Twitter, LinkedIn, Second Life or any other website that you can argue involves a virtual community. If you are not already a member of some sort of social networking site, you should temporarily enroll in one for the purposes of this question. How do the developers use software to mitigate against negative externalities in the VC and to enhance and bring out the benefits in the VC?

2 Staying with the virtual community that you chose in the previous question, describe the opportunities for advertising that exist in that community.

3 What should the host of a sponsored virtual community do if someone attacks the product? Should the company engage in censorship, and why or why not?

4 What do you think motivates consumers to create online word-of-mouth about the products they use?

5 Recall the notion of customer lifetime value that was introduced in Chapter 7. How could we modify the idea to take into account the likelihood that a consumer might recommend the product to others on social media?

REFERENCES

Bass, F.M. (1969), "A new product growth model for consumer durables," *Management Science*, **15**(5), 215–27.

Bauer, H.H. and M. Grether (2002), "Virtual communities and relationship marketing," Working Paper, University of Mannheim, Department of Marketing II, Germany.

Montgomery, A.L. (2001), "Applying quantitative marketing techniques to the Internet," *Interfaces*, **31** (2), 90–108.

Muñiz, A.M., Jr. and T.C. O'Guinn (2001), "Brand community," *Journal of Consumer Research*, **27** (4), 412–32.

O'Reilly, T. (2005), "What is Web 2.0? Design patterns and business models for the next generation of software," accessed October 10, 2008 at http://www.oreillynet.com/pub/a/oreilly/tim/news/2005/09/30/what-is-web-20.html.

Porter, C.E. (2004), "A typology of virtual communities: A multi-disciplinary foundation for future research," *Journal of Computer-Mediated Communication*, **10** (1), Article 3.

Szmigin, I. and A.E. Reppel (2004), "Internet community bonding: The case of Macnews.de," *European Journal of Marketing*, **38** (5/6), 626–40.

Villanueva, J., S. Yoo and D.M. Hanssens (2008), "The impact of marketing-induced versus word-of-mouth customer acquisition on customer equity growth," *Journal of Marketing Research*, **45** (1), 48–59.

25

Social media

In Chapter 24, we read of the importance of word-of-mouth to marketers. Social media serve to amplify consumer complaints. A study by Pew Internet (2012) shows us just how powerful this amplification can be, especially for younger people:

Source: Pew Internet (2012).

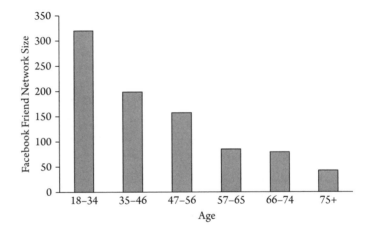

Figure 25.1 The number of Facebook friends you have depends on your age

According to Alexa (2017) some of the most popular websites in the world are social media sites. Facebook by itself has nearly 2 billion users (Sparks, 2017) – a clear indication that electronic services scale in a way that offline services cannot. A common question that companies ask is: how can my company use Facebook, Twitter, and other social media websites for business purposes? Companies are recognizing the tremendous growth rate of popular social sites. For example, Facebook currently boasts a user base exceeding 2.13 billion people (Facebook, 2018). It is a simple rule of marketing that the more people there are, the better the opportunity. By that rule, the opportunity in social media is truly immense. The problem is that few companies have much experience in how to use such media for marketing purposes. After some preliminary definitions, this chapter will present some real-world examples of success stories for companies using social media as a marketing medium.

What are social media?

Some authors have referred to social media as a revolution. Clara Shih's (2011) best-selling book *The Facebook Era* presents the idea that every decade a new technology appears that transforms the way companies conduct business. In the 1970s, the mainframe computer was used to automate company processes (see Chapter 6). The 1980s ushered in the personal computer, which brought information to the employee desktop. The 1990s introduced the Internet. According to Shih (2011), these three revolutions have now been followed by a fourth, namely social media. Of course, all revolutions have winners and losers. For the most part, companies that effectively adapted and managed the new technology were able to outperform rivals who were not as effective in doing so. So, we now return to our question. . . how can companies use it?

Before we can answer that question we ought to define it. In this book the word "network" has been used quite a bit. The original Web and its ability to link documents enabled a network of documents. So, using that terminology, we can think of any social medium as creating a World Wide Web of people. Given that, it is time to provide an official definition:

> A social medium is a software platform that specializes in connecting people, thereby creating a network where people are nodes, and connections between nodes tend to be social in nature.

So, now we have the addition of a Web of people to the original Web of sites. The Web of people reveals how folks are linked together by their interests, hobbies, and preferences, and with whom they share information and opinions. Of course, all this information is of interest to marketers.

You have no doubt noticed that the Facebook "Like" button frequently appears on web pages that are not directly affiliated with Facebook. When a consumer clicks the "Like" button, perhaps on a product page (i.e., a non-Facebook page), two things happen. First, that consumer's Facebook friends will see that he or she likes that particular product. Second, that "Like" is stored in Facebook's internal database about that consumer and the web page he or she was visiting. Facebook, or its clients, then can apply analytical modeling or data mining (see Chapter 7) to understand or discover patterns of consumer behavior – what sites they visit and what things they like – to allow firms to deliver the right content to the right consumer at the right time. Data mining can be used to simply count the number of mentions of your brand (buzz or word-of-mouth volume) or to detect the sentiment of the buzz or word-of-mouth (word-of-mouth valence). Here word-of-mouth valence refers to the distinction between positive word-of-mouth (with positive valence) and negative word-of-mouth (with negative valence). It is also possible to use data mining (in this case, specifically text mining) software to see what other words are placed near your brand's name. Facebook, with its knowledge of people's social networks, its reach and presence throughout the Web, and its massive archive of brand conversations, is becoming ever more important for marketing intelligence gathering.

So, with Facebook serving as a prototypical social medium, clearly one of the greatest ways that companies can use social is by utilizing data. In somewhat less technical terms, companies can listen to the conversation. There are many reasons to do so. We can generate sales leads. We can get new product ideas, or learn what our customers like. If customers complain we can learn where our staff need more training or where we need to apply a service recovery strategy. So let's talk about listening now.

Listen first, act second

A key principle for using social media is that the firm should not immediately jump into online conversations and make a hard sales pitch. Imagine that you are having a party at your house and you invite a friend who is a car dealer. What would be the reaction from the party-goers if your car dealer friend walked into the party talking through a megaphone to boast about all the great deals he can offer to everyone? For the most part, the other party-goers would be annoyed; and the marketing communication from the car dealer would be regarded as intrusive. This analogy carries over into social media. Consumers primarily use social sites as a means of personal communication with friends and family. A marketer from a company may be regarded initially as an outsider to a certain extent. Carefully and patiently allow consumers to speak to and about the company before entering the conversation. Listening first will enable a company to ascertain how they can offer some type of value to consumers. Communicating value instead of communicating an ad is best practice.

There is software outside of Facebook that can help marketers listen to the social landscape about a specific topic, product, or company. Google Alerts (http://www.google.com/alerts) is a free and easy-to-use tool that allows you to automate searches for keywords and phrases. You are alerted via email whenever Google indexes a web page that contains a keyword or phrase you have an interest in. This enables a marketer to quickly identify online content that discusses keywords of interest. In addition to Google Alerts there are several online tools that range from free to pay-for-use to monitor online conversations, such as Social Mention, Radian6 and others. Facebook, YouTube, and Twitter also have built-in analytics and advanced search features to help monitor what others are discussing. More advanced techniques allow for sentiment analysis, where software looks to count the co-occurrence of brand mentions with positive or negative terms.

The following sections illustrate how some companies have successfully engaged consumers in the context of social media. Engagement is a key principle here, which we will return to at the end of this chapter.

Jeep on Facebook

Jeep has created a large brand following on Facebook with over 1 million "Likes." Such a large following of consumers helps to generate conversation among them – a good example of externalities (see Chapter 23). Jeep often posts questions to consumers, which then generate two benefits. First, consumers discuss the questions, all the while interacting with other consumers, thereby increasing their engagement with the brand and the brand community (see Chapter 24 for more on communities). Second, by listening to these conversations, Jeep collects insights. For example, Jeep can capture opinions about what consumers like and dislike about their vehicles. Topics of discussion often include different types of vehicle options, tires, rims, accessories, and unofficial group events such as off-roading. Jeep can mine the comments to identify what consumers find interesting. Then Jeep can jump into conversations knowing that the topic of discussion is a relevant, valuable communication offering to consumers.

Dell and Moonfruit on Twitter

Some years back, Dell began to realize that some customers had grown dissatisfied with the company. Some of these customers were turning to Twitter to voice their complaints and warn other consumers about Dell's poor products and service. Dell assembled a team to monitor Twitter (and blogging sites) in an effort to respond in real time to negative comments. Now, the responses that Dell made to complaining consumers were not defensive in tone. Rather, the responses were caring and empathetic in an effort to win back those customers with effective service recovery (Chapter 2). Comcast, Lowe's, Tesco and Vodafone and other firms are similarly using Twitter for customer service.

Aside from customer service, Twitter can also be used for brand name awareness. Moonfruit is a small Web design software company that created a unique marketing campaign taking the form of a contest. An announcement about the contest was made to the company's 300 Twitter followers in 2009. The week-long contest would award two MacBook Airs per day among participants who tweeted "#moonfruit" (the hash tag # is used to identify a keyword of interest on Twitter). The details of this contest were simple: tweet #moonfruit as many times as you want and use the word any way you choose. It did not have to be about the company or the product. One tweet was chosen randomly per day to win a MacBook Air and another winner was selected per day that used what was judged to be the most creative use of #moonfruit. In one week the number of Twitter followers for the company grew from 300 to 47 000! At any given moment during the week, 5–10 percent of all tweets contained #moonfruit. This caused #moonfruit to become a trending topic, placing it on the home page of Twitter (for even more exposure to consumers). The positive results were not constrained to Twitter. Traffic to Moonfruit's website increased 1000 percent, leading to a 50 percent increase in free trial software downloads, and a 30 percent increase in sales. Interesting note: Twitter did not like what Moonfruit did and has since frowned upon other companies conducting similar contests. However, the key takeaway from this example is that Twitter can effectively create buzz surrounding a company or product.

LinkedIn

Like other social media, on this site humans are the nodes but here the links between the nodes represent professional or business connections. As such, LinkedIn appears to be custom made for business-to-business (B2B) relationships, as discussed in Chapter 8. One's LinkedIn network can serve as a very powerful sales tool. After all, a lot of traditional sales leads merely include the name, phone number and position held of the potential client. It is hard to make a cold call with just that basic information. In contrast, a wealth of information exists on LinkedIn such as mutual acquaintances, places of former employment, or interests, as revealed by LinkedIn groups. For example, if a salesperson has 300 people in their LinkedIn network, and those connections have an average of 90 people each in their own network, then the salesperson has 27 000 potential second-degree connections with the potential client.

LinkedIn is also a great way to find talent to strengthen a company's capabilities. LinkedIn serves as a valuable source of what has been called passive job candidates. These are people who may be happily employed and not specifically looking for work. The result is that a company is able to approach experienced workers at a fraction of the cost compared to traditional job placement or recruitment firms.

Advertising on social media

Chapter 14 discussed using YouTube for advertising. Here we briefly mention placing ads on social media websites. Since Facebook has such a detailed collection of information on its users, the Facebook ad interface enables a company to specify very specific characteristics of the intended target audience. For example, a company may prefer to only show their ad to Facebook users who are male, between the ages of 21 and 45 years old, and who live within 25 miles of Tallahassee, FL. Facebook immediately calculates the number of registered users who meet these criteria to give you an approximate idea of the reach of such target characteristics (approximately 57 000 users using the aforementioned criteria in this example). You can also choose to target other characteristics and demographics such as relationship status, languages, education, workplaces, and specific interests and hobbies.

Facebook allows you to set an ad budget to help you control costs. As is the case with Google search advertising, you only pay when a user clicks on your ad. It is important to note that the more specific your targeted audience is, the higher Facebook will charge you per ad click. This is due to the notion that a highly targeted audience has a greater chance to click your ad.

Engagement

Finally, one key use of social media by firms, by advertising or other means, is to generate consumer engagement. Engagement can take many forms, but active participation by consumers is the hallmark of engagement: retweeting, reposting, liking, commenting, check-ins, reviewing, tagging, uploading photos, and posting are all examples of engagement. In addition to advertising, questions, polls, contests and various forms of brand postings are ways that companies can engage their customers. The various kinds of postings that companies make are often collectively referred to as content and thus we often speak of content marketing.

Needless to say, we hope that the engagement we generate is positive, that it is motivated by positive attitudes towards our brand, but even negative engagement can be diagnostic for us and therefore useful. More than traditional advertising, the goal on social media is to create a conversation, a conversation we hope our customers will stay engaged with.

QUESTIONS AND EXERCISES

1 Briefly explain the difference between the World Wide Web of documents and the World Wide Web of people. How are these two different? How are they the same? Which one is more useful to marketers and why?

2 To begin this question, define the economic terms "substitute" and "complement." Now think about Facebook and Twitter. Does each act in the market for social media as a substitute for the other? Are they complements of each other? Of course, you should justify your answer.

3 The newest mobile devices consisting of smartphones and tablets have become very popular. Explain how these devices are helping, or if you prefer, hindering the growth of social media. Will mobile change the way social is used? Will mobile reduce or increase the importance of social to marketers and why?

4 If you are not already a user, learn about Foursquare. What do you think of Foursquare's value proposition? Do you like what the firm offers? Would you or would you not wish to join the service? Explain why.

5 If you are not already a user, learn about Groupon. What do you think of Groupon's value proposition? Do you like what the firm offers? Would you or would you not wish to join the service? Explain why.

6 If you are not already a user, sign up for Klout. What is your Klout score? In the next two weeks, can you drive your score up by your use of Facebook, Twitter, Google+, and other social media?

 REFERENCES

Alexa (2017), "Alexa top 500 global sites," accessed July 27, 2017 at http://www.alexa.com/topsites.

Facebook (2018), Facebook company info page, accessed February 6, 2018 at https://newsroom.fb.com/company-info/.

Pew Internet (2012), "Facebook: A profile of its 'friends'," *Tumblr Data Posting*, accessed December 18, 2018 at http://pewinternet.tumblr.com/post/23177613721/facebook-a-profile-of-its-friends-in-light-of.

Shih, C. (2011), *The Facebook Era*, Englewood Cliffs, NJ: Prentice Hall.

Sparks, D. (2017), "How many users does Facebook have?", *Motley Fool*, March 30, accessed September 27, 2017 at https://www.fool.com/investing/2017/03/30/how-many-users-does-facebook-have.aspx.

26

Strategy in a networked world

The goal of this chapter is to put together some of the themes discussed in previous chapters, and to provide an overview of digital marketing strategy. The way we do this is by setting up an argument: is marketing the same today as it was before the advent of the Internet, or has the explosion of technology changed marketing in a fundamental way?

Marketing is the same

Every generation believes that the time in which it lives is unique. But can we really assert that *Angry Birds* is a more radical invention than the telegraph? When cities began to connect to each other by telegraph in the nineteenth century, for the first time in human history, information could reliably travel faster than a horse. Can we seriously claim that the "Like" button is a more radical invention than the printing press? After the invention of the printing press in the fifteenth century, for the first time in history ordinary people could afford books.

Alert students may have already noticed that this textbook on digital marketing includes many of the concepts from an Introduction to Marketing course. We have talked about service and satisfaction, and about segmentation and search. Section II reviewed many of the important principles of advertising, while Section III reviewed many classic topics taught in retailing. This could lead us to conclude that marketing is little changed by the recent proliferation of electronic services. In this view, just because we add the word "digital" in front of the word "marketing" does not change the fact that we are still doing marketing. Next, you will see a list of many other core ideas of marketing and you will note that they may be used to buttress this viewpoint.

Marketing remains a game of coordinating the firm's efforts at branding and positioning the offering while differentiating it from competitive offers. Knowledge about the customer market remains critical in doing so. Our knowledge about the market allows us to break that market into segments and to serve each segment better with a customized offering. The fact that an online newspaper can perform mass customization on its offering, allowing each reader to have his or her own version of the paper, is essentially a continuation of the notion of segmentation. The fact that Google and Facebook are high-tech services is unimportant. What is important is that these are valuable brands that are perfectly positioned for competitive advantage in the segments they serve.

Relationships have been identified as critical in marketing long before addressable media like the Internet evolved to allow us to engage our customers one-on-one and evaluate the profitability of that relationship. The fact that Amazon leverages online data and consumer-generated reviews to better compete is irrelevant. What is important is that Amazon is adept at the old-fashioned skill of relationship marketing.

Historically, marketers have always needed to think through what the outcome variable is. This is still true today in online marketing. What is the goal? How do we measure progress towards it? Share? Profit? Sales? Unique visitors? These questions are classic marketing questions, and are, if anything, even more important today. Online or offline, it still makes sense for marketers to understand the relationship between decision variables (factors that they control) and outcome variables like those listed above. Decision variables frequently involve the 4Ps (product, price, promotion and place) and can include any aspect of website design. Analytical modeling in marketing has been around for many decades and is even more feasible in today's world awash in digital data. Consumer psychologists might suggest that the heuristics and biases of the human mind are the same whether that mind is confronted by a screen or a piece of paper.

Marketers still need to scan the environment: the regulatory environment, the competitive environment, the consumer environment and the internal company environment. Electronic networks make scanning easier, thus reinforcing the rule and rewarding marketers even more for paying attention to the marketing environment.

Whether we think that offline marketing is different than online marketing or not, it is surely critical that marketers fully integrate their offline and online efforts. The challenges of integrating all distributional efforts are described in Chapter 17, in the section on multichannel retailing. Likewise, maintaining a consistent promotional and branding message across all media types is a key consideration. There are now many new ways of touching the customer. Surely marketing planning and control has got harder and thus more important in separating winners and losers in the race to better satisfy customers.

Now you have seen some strong arguments that ought to convince you that marketing is the same. Let's see what the arguments are that marketing is different.

Marketing is different

To make the argument that marketing is different now, here is a list of industries that in recent years have been hit with a wave of technology-induced disruption. The music industry has fought file copying and while it keeps winning in the courts it keeps losing in the stores. The movie industry is now facing similar pressure – fans are copying and sharing popular films. Newspaper circulations are down, and their one big source of revenue, classified ads, is being hammered by Craigslist and other e-services. The book industry now faces the biggest change since Gutenberg, as Sony and Amazon have redesigned the distribution channel with the invention of the electronic book. The encyclopedia business is now gone thanks to Wikipedia. It is an understatement to note that the business model of Wikipedia is very different than the business model of the *Encyclopædia Britannica*! Real estate agencies, home town stock brokerages, corner video rental stores, and many other industries have basically become extinct in the past few years due to online competition. The entire retailing ecology has been perturbed by the advent of new mobile – and addressable – distribution channels. Who will be the next victims? Wearable devices are growing in popularity. What firms will those kill? The advent of 3D printing may leave a lot of dead companies in its wake.

If nothing has changed, how did all of the expert marketers in all of these businesses completely fail? They have all been beaten at their own game by new, technologically adept market entrants. The new players, from Amazon and iTunes through Zazzle and Zillow, were not satisfied with playing the game better. They changed the rules of the marketing game.

Generals, it is claimed, are always fighting the last war. If you are on top of the market, why should you change your approach? Your employees have a set of capabilities that have worked in the past. These tendencies lead to inertia on the part of incumbent firms. In addition, firms within a sector are susceptible to mimetic pressure, which is another way to say that firms tend to imitate each other.

Firms within an industry tend to fall in love with what they do best. The music industry was good at producing disks. Perhaps we should not be surprised that it was Apple who figured out how to sell music online. The book industry was good at producing paper products. Perhaps we should not be surprised that it was Amazon who figured out how to sell digitized books. The newspaper business was good at dropping paper on your doorstep each morning. Perhaps we should not be surprised that a group of techies in San Francisco took away their classified advertisement revenue. All the winners in these battles – Apple, Amazon, Craigslist – are firms that were born digital.

It is always difficult for the incumbent to produce a new product that makes the incumbent's old product obsolete. Who within the firm is going to support pouring money into such a new product? Certainly, people whose career has been rewarded by supporting the old product are not motivated to destroy that product. Few companies have the stomach to "eat their own children." Perhaps the most famous example of a company that destroys the immediate-term revenue-earning capabilities of its own products is Intel. Intel will ruthlessly introduce a new generation of chips even while the previous generation is still earning massive revenue. This puts a damper on sales of the previous generation of chips in the short run but enhances the long-term prospects for the company. Intel is a technology company. It is doubtful that this is a coincidence. Other companies tend to be too afraid to do it.

In addition to the changes in retailing, let's think about what has happened to advertising. We could make the argument that advertising has been turned completely upside down by technology. In the beginning, we marketers were able to force our messages on an unwilling audience. Then came the remote control device, video cassette recorders, TiVo and now digital video recorders. Consumers can zap or zip through the commercials at will. Likewise, direct telephone calls to the consumer have been defeated by answering machines and voice mail. At the beginning of the Internet, it looked like pop-ups might allow us to retain some power to put messages in the face of the unwilling consumer. Then the browsers started to incorporate pop-up blockers. Now we have user-generated content. It is the consumer who has taken the initiative to blog, update and upload about brands they hate or love. It appears that advertising has indeed been turned upside down.

The above paragraphs list some evidence for serious change, but you may not have been convinced that marketing is different now. The trend towards user-generated content certainly implies that something is different. It further suggests that the consumer has been empowered as never before (Deighton and Kornfeld, 2009). That leads us to wrap up this chapter by discussing the role of marketing in an era of powerful consumers.

Marketing's role in organizations

Despite the list of marketing failures that began this chapter, let us not think that marketing is in bad shape today. If we accept the notion that the consumer has been empowered by communications technology such as blogs, social bookmarking sites, Twitter, Facebook and other platforms that allow user-generated content, this should work to the advantage of marketing. As the discipline that spans the boundary between the firm and the customer, to the extent that the customer has more power, this expands the role and importance of marketing within the firm. The content that users are creating helps marketers even more. Users suggest new product lines, advertising strategies, and let us know when our service could be improved. Our brands will benefit from a more active contribution by a consumer who is, after all, communicating with the world using what amounts to a supercomputer, or what would have been a supercomputer a few decades ago. Our role as marketers is to integrate our firms' need to make a profit, along with the consumers' need to be treated as an equal, in the networked system that connects us all together.

 QUESTIONS AND EXERCISES

1 Does the consumer really have more power, or are huge corporations more powerful than ever? Pick a specific industry and make your argument.
2 This question repeats a question from Chapter 1. Now that you have read almost the entire book, do a competitive analysis of two websites where the products or services in question are in direct competition. For example, Coke vs Pepsi, Ford vs Chevy, Delta vs United Airlines, Hilton vs Marriott, Eveready vs Duracell, Gatorade vs Lucozade, FedEx vs UPS, or any other pair of competitors that you can think of.
3 This chapter, as well as Chapter 22, uses the expression "business model." Define the expression. Has the Internet enabled brand new types of business models? Or has the Internet merely led previously rare business models to become commonplace?
4 Is marketing different now, or the same?

 REFERENCE

Deighton, J. and L. Kornfeld (2009), "Interactivity's unanticipated consequences for marketers and marketing," *Journal of Interactive Marketing*, **23** (1), 4–10.

27

The future of e-marketing

> Prediction is very difficult, especially if it's about the future.
> (Niels Bohr)

In this chapter, we are going to contemplate a set of technological trends that seem to have characterized the last several decades, and to think about what might happen if these trends continue for the next several decades. First, there is the increase in computational power per dollar that we see in hardware. Second, the speed at which these hardware devices are connected, called bandwidth, is increasing. Third, there is the increasing portability or mobility of many types of hardware devices. Fourth, we are accumulating a heritage of software that underpins the value of the other trends. Finally, the fifth and last trend is the movement towards more network connectivity.

Our task in this chapter is to try to imagine what the business world will be like after these trends have run for another pair of decades – about the time you and your classmates will be well into your careers.

Hardware

The most famous law describing hardware trends is named after US engineer Gordon Moore, one of the co-founders of the Intel Corporation. In a 1965 article in *Electronics* magazine, he noted that the number of transistors on a computer chip had doubled every 18–24 months since the invention of the integrated circuit in 1958. What made this explosion in circuit complexity possible was the steadily shrinking size of transistors over the decades. Since 1965, Moore's Law has taken on a sort of life of its own due to input from others and has now come to encompass a whole list of hardware components that behave in a similar manner, including the number of transistors per chip, hard disk and random access memory capacity and the number of pixels per dollar. In its most general form, analysts speak of the doubling of computational power per dollar over a fixed time period.

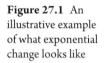

Figure 27.1 An illustrative example of what exponential change looks like

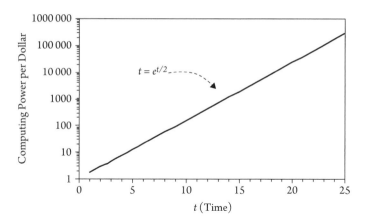

Note that when we say that something doubles every 18 months we are saying that there is a constant percentage change (100 percent increase) during each 18-month period, year in and year out. If capacity starts as 1, when it doubles it becomes $1{\cdot}2 = 2^1 = 2$. Another doubling takes it $2{\cdot}2 = 2^2 = 4$. A third doubling yields $2^3 = 8$. You can see the pattern – the amount of time that passes ends up as an exponent. A constant percentage change is therefore also called exponential change. A graph illustrating exponential growth appears in Figure 27.1. Unless you scale the y-axis on a log scale, the graph will tend to go almost straight up. A log scale means that in effect, all we do on the y-axis is count zeros.

Engineers and industry analysts believe that Moore's Law will continue to operate over the next couple of decades, creating ever more capable and smaller chips. So, can we predict that within 20 years your computer will become as small as a pinhead? For one thing, it would be pretty hard to type on it and to read the screen at that size, no? Obviously just because we can make something tiny does not mean we have to do so. We can always add a little bulk. This suggests that since hardware can be made to any arbitrary size, it is ultimately the human body, and mind, that will determine what our hardware will look and feel like. For an historical example, note that the physical form of a credit card is based solely on human convenience. Anything larger would be slightly harder to carry, while anything smaller would tend to get lost or dropped. Thus, to predict what devices will look like, we ought to think about the size of the human hand, the acuity of the human eye, the sensitivity of the human ear, the understanding of the human mind, and the desires of the human heart.

And speaking of desire, a trend that started with telephony in Europe and Asia, is that hardware offerings are increasingly turning into expressive products. One's choice of phone is no longer determined by purely technical factors, but by what that phone says about us, how attractive it looks, its hedonic properties, and, simply put, how cool it is. The same factors have figured heavily in the growth of Apple iPhone sales. This trend towards technology as costume will presumably accelerate as devices come to be built into clothing or jewelry. In general, we might expect devices to get closer to the body. Headphones have become lighter and smaller and have evolved into ear buds. Monitors have become flatter. Computer input has gone from heavy steel keypunch machines to voice-activated wearable microphones.

Would you be willing to have a miniature microphone attached to the back of a tooth to achieve 24/7 hands-free cell phone talking, including access to emergency services and Google? And what if an infinitesimally small ear bud could be affixed to the inside of your ear, invisible and so light that you couldn't feel it? You would never have to carry a phone around with you.

If we earn the customer's trust, digital marketing could involve far more intimate relationships than it does today. The potential for very close relationships with customers will emerge as devices move closer to the body, but the privacy challenges of such relationships will require careful attention to the inevitable ethical issues that will arise. The possibility of new personal electronic services is obvious but these services will require clear-headed ethical thinking.

Bandwidth

At higher connection speeds, the quantity and the quality of information sent around a network change. Daft and Lengel (1986) make a clear distinction between the amount of information and the richness of that information. They call their approach media richness theory. According to this theory, there are two types of problem solving:

- **Uncertainty reduction**, where uncertainty is characterized by the absence or insufficiency of information: It can be reduced by collecting or receiving more information. In other words, uncertainty can be solved by upping the quantity of information. For example, if I do not know if my customers like the color of my product, I can ask three potential customers if they like it, but my estimate of the market reaction would be quite uncertain. On the other hand, if I ask 1000 customers, I could greatly reduce that uncertainty.
- **Equivocality reduction**, where an equivocality is a confusion or ambi-

guity surrounding a topic area: If not knowing how many people will like a blue product represents uncertainty, equivocality would occur if we are not sure what product markets we should be in and what our goals might be in those markets. Such issues are often called ill-defined questions. We reduce equivocality through debate, clarification, and by coming to a consensus interpretation of our business situation.

We reduce uncertainty when we increase the amount of information that a medium can handle, but we can only reduce equivocality by increasing the richness of the medium. The richness is determined by a medium's capacity for feedback, personalization and the number of channels (e.g., text, voice, video) it can carry. As a medium adds channels, it increasingly resembles live, natural face-to-face conversation.

This suggests that as digital media like the Internet become richer, the kinds of consumer problem solving, and the kinds of business-to-business (B2B) cooperation that these media can support will expand. Right now, consumer use of the Internet peaks during the search stage of consumer problem solving. Richer media might enhance use at the problem recognition stage, and also change the nature of the evaluation process, making it deeper and more effective. It might also become more critical during post-purchase evaluation as consumers could better convey their product experience to others.

In terms of B2B decision making, we should note that firms tend to possess two different kinds of information (Nahapiet and Ghoshal, 1998):

- **Codifiable information**, consisting of routines that can easily be described in words that help to coordinate employees: "When a customer is ready to pay, ask them if they want fries with their order."
- **Tacit knowledge:** Information that is not so easily described, and which is sometimes also referred to as know-how. Tacit knowledge is typically acquired through experience; that is, learning by doing, and thus cannot easily be acquired by competing firms. It is especially important for innovation. Tacit knowledge can form the basis of firm capabilities, a topic we covered in Chapter 6 on internal company operations.

We may hypothesize that as digital networks become richer, tacit knowledge will begin to more easily flow through them, adding flexibility and volatility to the competitive landscape. Cooperation within supply chains may also become deeper.

Mobility

Increasing mobility is a by-product of Moore's Law, discussed above, but mobility requires one extra factor: battery power. Thus, a key limiting technology pertains to the portable delivery of the power needed to run mobile devices. There is a tremendous race taking place right now among venture capitalists to find and fund new battery technologies. As batteries get smaller and more powerful, watch for the mobile devices, discussed in Chapter 18, becoming increasingly important in marketing. As batteries improve, assisted by kinetic energy (using your motion), what we think of as a gadget will get smaller and be able to blend in with clothes, or the body itself, or masquerade as jewelry. Other potential gadgets might resemble tattoos or be implanted in teeth. If this sounds fanciful, note that in the 1960s, the television screen was 5 meters away. In the 1980s the PC screen was 1 meter away. Now the iPhone is in your pocket and its earbuds are, well, literally in your ears. The trend seems clear: stuff is getting closer to the body.

It seems that not a year goes by without the introduction of a new type of mobile device. We have seen smartphones, tablets and e-readers in rapid succession. Given this innovation we might conclude that even though the Web is the hub of multichannel retailing activity today, mobile will eventually take over that role. The power of the mobile hub will grow as mobile networks become more open, and therefore more able to take advantage of software communities. Let's talk about software next.

Software

The difference between hardware and software is roughly analogous to the difference between a good and a service. Hardware is tangible, concrete and visual while software performs an action on behalf of the user. It is also the case that there is no software equivalent to Moore's Law. Software generally moves forward in small incremental steps, but also occasionally yields surprising leaps forward. It is quite possible that the very term "electronic marketing" predisposes us to think that hardware (i.e., electronic devices) is the only key to what is happening in technology. Perhaps a better term than electronic marketing would be "software-mediated marketing" but it is pretty doubtful that such a phrase would catch on. For this book I have compromised and used the term digital marketing.

Let's take a look at the most recent history of the Internet, looking for software innovations that were not present in the beginning, in the 1990s, but which have now become increasingly relevant in digital marketing:

- **Blogs:** In the 1990s, only a handful of people had a home page but now several million people blog. The difference between a home page and a blog is fairly subtle. A blog is very much like a home page, but the blog editing software automatically creates a chronological structure featuring the current edition of your blog, with previous editions archived but still available. This changes the nature of the content that people generate from static to dynamic. A chronological structure also encourages the user to constantly update and thereby create more content as compared to a home page.

- **RSS:** This acronym stands for Really Simple Syndication and has created a second "push" option for the Internet, after email. And unlike email, at least so far, RSS has not been afflicted with a spam problem. In addition to RSS, platforms such as Facebook also produce similar feeds.

- **Wikipedia:** The software that runs wiki platforms starts with a simple imperative: make it as easy to create content as it is to read it. Add to that an ability to see and revert to previous versions of the content, and you have in Wikipedia one of the most visited sites on the Internet. In wikis, we see software mitigating against negative externalities (in the form of spam or non-consensual posting) and also reducing the cost side of the content generation equation.

- **Intelligent agents:** These are autonomous software entities capable of searching for information, and acting on it. They are used to help us search, compare, prioritize, negotiate, buy, collaborate, adapt and learn. Some examples include eBay's ShopBot, mySimon, and Kelkoo. It does appear, however, that intelligent agents have not yet caught on as a mass Web phenomenon.

- **SETI@home:** Unfortunately for astronomers, analyzing radio signals from telescopes takes a lot of supercomputer time, which is quite expensive. That is why astronomers at Berkeley came up with an alternative. You can download a screensaver that performs work while you are away from the computer. As of February, 2018, the software is said to have over 5 million participants worldwide (Wikipedia, 2018). As we reach the end of the day in North America, and people go to bed, machines there begin to work on the computations. Later, as Asia goes to bed, the action shifts westward. Later still, the Europeans get sleepy and walk away from their computers, and then the cycle returns to North America.

Of course, we have left out many other interesting software innovations from the above list such as Twitter, reddit, Digg, Flickr, Snapchat and others. One thing that we can say though is that many of these programs share a common theme. Blogs empower ordinary people to write and express their opinions rather than passively reading the opinions of elite, professional writers. Even a small-time blog can be followed with RSS. Wikipedia enables users to create and edit knowledge products, intelligent agents allow consumers to effortlessly process product information and SETI@home allows people with ordinary PCs to combine their computing power to create the equivalent of a super-computer. Surely this is an important theme that will continue into the future, that the kind of power in the hands of the consumer will continue to grow.

None of the software innovations described above would happen without the network connections that allow collaboration, and it is to this topic that we now turn.

Networks

As we learned in the discussion of externalities in Chapter 23, as networks get larger, they tend to become more valuable for everybody. The SETI@home project shows us that this value can occur in unexpected ways. Sticking with the astronomy theme, the clickworkers project demonstrates that a problem that can only be solved with the human mind and some human labor is also susceptible to collaborative action, only in this case we refer to it as crowd-sourcing. NASA needed to identify craters in a minutely detailed map of Mars that had been sent back to Earth by the Mars orbiter. NASA therefore asked volunteers to look over small pieces of that map to try to find craters. Thus, a huge, labor-intensive job got solved by hundreds of thousands of people, five minutes at a time.

Another example of network-enabled collaboration comes from St. John's University, New York, where Professor of Management Charles Wankel sought to create a new type of management textbook with hundreds of coauthors, each writing a small portion of the text (Wankel, 2011). If that example, is too, well, academic, consider the *World of Warcraft* game, in which thousands of players collaborate to have fun, playing an online game together. New models of human interaction become possible as we connect ourselves.

Another example of the power of the network relates to auctions, covered in Chapter 20. Chen and Plott (2002) describe the ways in which markets can function as highly accurate information aggregation mechanisms and how Hewlett Packard leveraged this to generate better sales predictions for a particular new product. Hewlett Packard created an internal market, setting up a series of securities, sort of like stock shares, that corresponded to different sales predictions. One stock would pay off if HP sold between 0 and 1500 units, another might pay off if HP sold between 1501 and 1600, and so forth. If the actual outcome fell within the range of that security, the security paid $1. Each territorial sales representative received some cash and an endowment of securities, and then the buying and selling began. In effect, the price of the security represents the probability of occurrence of the outcome encoded by that security and the market functions as a prediction market. There are also public prediction markets such as Intrade, and the Iowa Electronic Markets. These exchanges have been quite accurate at predicting US election results.

Electronic networks have shown themselves to be quite useful in enhancing many pre-existing marketing activities such as promotion and retailing. Such networks create addressable, interactive promotional media ideal for relationships. Electronic networks can also create a substitute or complementary distribution channel. But networks are also used to create brand new electronic services that have not existed previously. As these networks become more ubiquitous and capable, it seems possible that we will see many new electronic services based on connecting people, businesses, ideas, work and play.

So now, having looked at the trends operating in recent history, it is time to make some global predictions. What will it be like when there are 100 billion supercomputers, many of these small and close to our person? We presume that these will be sending and receiving user-generated as well as client–server content and offering new services via rich media, all connected at high speed with software that allows us to do together what we really can't do alone. What indeed will happen?

That takes us back to the Niels Bohr quote at the beginning of this chapter. Sometimes it is hard to predict what happens when a system of agents becomes connected as network nodes. In this case we humans – hedonic or utilitarian – and our computing devices – home-, office-based, or mobile – are the agents. Even if we perfectly understand these agents, the behavior of the overall network may not be predictable. The organization that results may not be apparent from properties of the agents. The level of complexity that emerges may dwarf the complexity of the sum of the parts. You cannot predict the psychology of a person knowing only the biology of that person's brain cells. You cannot predict the economic behavior of a market knowing only the psychology of the buyers and sellers. Sometimes properties emerge in a surprising way. Such emergent properties may surprise us. In fact, we should be surprised if we are not surprised by the future.

QUESTIONS AND EXERCISES

1 If the chips and other hardware that go into a camera can be made arbitrarily small, how would you go about designing the camera around the human user? How big would it be? What shape would it be?

2 As media become richer, will there be any purpose to face-to-face business interaction? If I can use an extremely high-resolution wall-sized display that can fool the eye into believing the other party is in the room with me, do I need to meet with that person in person? Assuming that touch is relatively irrelevant to business communication, would face-to-face meetings become basically obsolete? Why or why not?

3 In the section on intelligent agents, what is meant by the word agent? In the section on emergent properties, what is meant there by the word agent? Hint: the latter example is closer to the notion of an economic agent.

4 Why do you suppose that intelligent agents and shopbots are not used by very many consumers during shopping?

5 As one moves around town, or the world, it is very handy to be able to consume or use certain benefits. From time to time when I am out and about, I might wish to take a picture, make a phone call, look at a video, listen to music, hear or see a transmission from a live sporting event, figure out where I am, send or receive text messages, check my email and perhaps send an email, and browse the Web. It would certainly be nice to have a single device that does all these things, but in general, there is a tradeoff between general devices that do many things fairly well and specialized devices that do a single thing very, very well. What will we be carrying around in our pockets in 15 years? One device? Many devices? If many, what will they specialize in?

REFERENCES

Chen, K.-Y. and C.R. Plott (2002), "Information aggregation mechanisms: Concept, implementation, and design for a sales forecasting problem," *Social Sciences Working Papers*, Division of the Humanities and the Social Sciences, California Institute of Technology.

Daft, R.L. and R.H. Lengel (1986), "Organizational information requirements, media richness and structural design," *Management Science*, **32** (5), 554–71.

Nahapiet, J. and S. Ghoshal (1998), "Social capital, intellectual capital, and the organizational advantage," *Academy of Management Review*, **23** (2), 242–66.

Wankel, C. (2011), *Management Through Collaboration: Teaming in a Networked World*, accessed February 6, 2018 at http://www.allbookstores.co.uk/book/0415992346/Management_through_Collaboration_Teaming_in_a_Networked_World.html.

Wikipedia (2018), "SETI@home" entry, accessed February 4, 2018 at http://en.wikipedia.org/wiki/SETI@home.

Index